Introduction to Poetics

Theory and History of Literature

Edited by Wlad Godzich and Jochen Schulte-Sasse

Volume 1. Tzvetan Todorov, *Introduction to Poetics*

Introduction

to

Poetics

Tzvetan Todorov

Translation from the French by Richard Howard

Introduction by Peter Brooks

Theory and History of Literature, Volume 1

University of Minnesota Press, Minneapolis

Originally published in French in *Qu'est-ce que le
structuralisme: Poétique* and later in a revised edition,
Poétique. ©1968, 1973 Éditions du Seuil.

Library of Congress Cataloging in Publication Data

Todorov, Tzvetan, 1939-
    Introduction to poetics.

    (Theory and history of literature; v. 1)
    Translation of: Poétique.
    Includes bibliographical references and index.
    1. Poetics.   2. Structuralism (Literary
analysis) I. Title. II. Series.
PN1043.T613 808.1   81-3073
ISBN 0-8166-1008-8   AACR2
ISBN 0-8166-1011-8 (pbk.)

Contents

Introduction
Peter Brooks

Literary criticism has in our century become a professional activity as never before, and in the past two decades there has been a remarkable resurgence of interest in understanding the bases of this activity—in the theory of literary discourse, or poetics. Few theorists and critics have contributed more lucidly, consistently, and usefully to the constitution of a new poetics than Tzvetan Todorov. His importance derives in part from his intellectual cosmopolitanism. Based in Paris, and owing much to the master of modern French criticism, Roland Barthes, Todorov also commands the Slavic tradition, Russian Formalism and the work of the Prague Linguistic Circle (he is Bulgarian by birth), and the Anglo-American New Criticism, as well as the seminal texts of German Romanticism. He stands as an important figure of transmission and integration, someone whose reach toward a poetics of the greatest generality is informed by a grasp of the diverse traditions of literary theory since Aristotle.

Todorov has presented elements of poetics in a wide-ranging series of books, inaugurated by his important anthology of Russian Formalist writings, *Théorie de la littérature* (Editions of Seuil, 1965), and including the much-cited study of the "fantastic," *Introduction à la littérature fantastique* (Seuil, 1970; published in English translation as *The Fantastic: A Structural Approach to a*

Literary Genre [The Press of Case Western Reserve University, 1973; Cornell Paperbacks, 1975]), the narrative theory of *Grammaire du Décaméron* (Mouton, 1969) and *Poétique de la prose* (Seuil, 1971; translated as *The Poetics of Prose* [Cornell, 1977]), and, more recently, *Théories du symbole* (Seuil, 1977), *Symbolisme et interprétation* (Seuil, 1978), and *Les Genres du discours* (Seuil, 1978); and he is also one of the founders and editors of *Poétique*, a journal that has become a vital international forum for literary criticism and theory. The present volume, *Introduction to Poetics*, which was originally a chapter of a collective volume called *Qu'est-ce que le structuralisme?* (Seuil, 1968) and then, completely revised, became a separate volume, *Poétique* (Seuil, 1973), occupies a special place in his work since it represents an effort at synthesis, presenting the principles of a contemporary poetics in brief, introductory, and at the same time comprehensive form.

Why poetics? The dream of a cogent theory of literature, Todorov notes at the outset of this volume, is almost as old as literature itself. In the Western tradition, the point of first reference is ever and still Aristotle, because his manner of proceeding, in laying out the properties and the parts of tragedy and epic, remains exemplary. Aristotle provides knowledge of literature, not simply commentary on it or information about it, in an organizing discourse derived from the study of literature itself rather than any branch of knowledge external to it. In our time, the call to poetics was forcefully sounded by Northrop Frye in his "Polemical Introduction" to *Anatomy of Criticism* (1957), where he deplored the futility of an ever-multiplying interpretive criticism that was not informed and organized by "a coherent and comprehensive theory of literature, logically and scientifically organized." That is, literary criticism (and literary pedagogy) should not be simply the explication and interpretation of texts *in vacuo,* where the only common ground of critic and reader is their mutual interest in literature, but rather a discipline in its own right, whose principles and organizing features can be discovered and systematically presented. "To defend the right of criticism to exist at all," wrote Frye, "is to assume that criticism is a structure of thought and knowledge existing in its own right, with some measure of independence from the art it deals with."

Here in essence is the double thrust of the argument for poetics: that on the one hand poetics should be a discipline derived from the study of literature, not some other field of knowledge that claims to explain literature, and on the other hand that the discipline of literary study must not simply assume that its justification and its coherence derive from the works that it studies, that it can be the sum of interpretations of individual literary works. Poetics must offer a systematic understanding of literary discourse as that which comprehends its individual manifestations, and it must understand in systematic fashion its own discourse on literature. Thus Todorov distinguishes from the interpretation of texts the *science* of literature, intending by the word "science" not to claim a degree of exactitude comparable to that achieved in the natural sciences, but to indicate a concern with the coherence of the body of knowledge and the principles of knowing that constitute literary study. Poetics hence is not "the description of the particular work, the designation of its meaning, but the establishment of general laws of which the particular text is the product." To those practitioners of literary interpretation who shudder at the claim to "science"—or find it pretentious—Todorov would, in the wake of Barthes, reply that any act of interpretation implies a theory of *how* texts mean—a poetics—that is usually unconscious and inchoate; and that the raison d'être of poetics is to make explicit and rational, and to test the coherence of, the theories that enable interpretation to take place. That interpreters can argue about what texts mean indicates that they have some notion that there are proper grounds for the production of meaning. But in common practice they signally fail to ask what makes their claims to meaning possible.

The revival of poetics in which Todorov has so fruitfully participated owes much to the large movement in the social sciences known as "structuralism," and particularly structuralism in linguistics. An earlier version of Todorov's *Poetics,* we noted, appeared in a volume that considered the meaning and the contribution of structuralism in the fields of linguistics, anthropology, philosophy, and psychoanalysis, as well as literary theory. One could say both that it is in structuralist thought that poetics has found the strongest impulse to its reformulation since perhaps the

Renaissance, and that it is in poetics that structuralist thought about literature finds its appropriate field of exercise. For in all fields, structuralism is properly concerned with the systematic functioning of the basic units and relations that define the production of meaning: the set of rules and operations in terms of which individual phenomena, or actions, come to signify.

The lessons of modern linguistics have been crucial to the development of poetics in this regard. For linguistics is concerned not with the interpretation or decoding of the individual utterance, but with the laws, conventions, operations that allow meaningful utterance to take place and to be understood. The fundamental distinctions made by Ferdinand de Saussure at the inception of modern linguistics remain exemplary for structuralist poeticians: the distinction between diachronic or evolutionary study on the one hand, and on the other hand synchronic study, which considers only the state of the system at a given moment—cuts a horizontal slice through it—and brackets considerations of evolution; the distinction between *langue* and *parole,* or system and its actualization in the speech act, and the decision that the former, the system and its vitualities of meaning, should be the object of scientific study. The Danish linguist Louis Hjelmslev summarized the position succinctly in his *Prolegomena to a Theory of Language:* "A priori it would seem to be a generally valid thesis that for every *process* there is a corresponding *system,* by which the process can be analyzed and described by means of a limited number of premises." As *langue* stands to *parole,* system to process, so should *poetics* stand to *interpretation,* acts of literary criticism: it is this study of the systematics of literature that poetics, on the model of linguistics, takes to be its object of attention.

Furthermore, Saussure considers that language is *form* rather than *substance,* a systematic set of relations in which what matters is not entities but the differences between them. If Saussure can make the claim that in language there are no positive values, only differences, he can do so because nothing in language means per se —language is not a nomenclature, a naming of the world—but only by distinctive opposition to something else within the system of differences that is language as a whole. The differential system of language works at all levels, from the elementary oppositions of phonemes and morphemes, to lexical and semantic differences, where difference is ever the way of ordering the field of the signifiable. In addition, the same rules of operation (and of analysis) obtain at every level of language, where we find associative and combinatorial relations among units, or, as they have come to be called since Saussure, *paradigmatic* and *syntagmatic* relations. The paradigmatic axis offers a set of equivalent elements, defined by similarity and difference, from which a selection is made and the elements selected then combined on the syntagmatic axis in a new whole—which can then be a paradigmatic element on the next higher level. With a limited set of operatory principles, then, one can move from the most elementary to the most complex levels of language (and vice versa) with perfect analytic pertinence.

So it is that linguistics offers the literary poetician a seductive model of total coherence and analytic power that seems more useful than anything that Frye (to return to that example) has at his command. Frye asserts that literary theory must elaborate "a conceptual framework derivable from an inductive survey of the literary field." Todorov's poetics, while surely informed by survey of the literary field, works nearly on a deductive hypothesis which is furnished by the laws and procedures of linguistics and which takes as its object not only existing works but those "virtual works" theoretically derivable from the laws of the system, literary discourse, as a whole. For his object of attention, once again, is not instances of meaning but the possibility of meaning: the ways in which the system allows meaning to be made.

As Todorov argues in the present volume, no doubt another field of scientific investigation could have offered poetics a model consonant with that it derived from linguistics. And yet, the authority of the linguistic model would seem to be supported by at least two powerful reasons. First, linguistics has in our century been the most impressive of the "sciences of man" in creating a scientific organization for itself, and on this basis making remarkable progress in the understanding of linguistic phenomena. Second, that linguistics speaks of language, the very medium of literature, has held a certain promise that its discoveries could be pertinent to the study of literature; and although—as Todorov notes—this is quite a different kind of usefulness from the provision of a model of analysis, in practice there has been an effect of reinforcement of the model by the material with which it deals. Saussure, after all, foresaw that linguistics would one day be only a branch of a larger field, semiotics—the general science of signs—and literature is in some sense (yet to be defined) a subset or a special case of the general system of signs.

But perhaps most important of all in the linguistic model is the lesson it offers in the possibilities of what one might call the formalist imagination: the analytic progress that can be achieved from the thoroughgoing formalization of a field of study. Paul Valéry, who spent much of his poetic career in meditation on the creative possibilities of such formal conventions as meter, once remarked: "What is form for others is subject matter for me." Here is the formalist gesture in essence: turning form into the object of reflection, bracketing questions of evolution and abstracting individual utterances so that the formal interrelationships of the field under study come into focus.

Yet the model of Saussurian linguistics—and its furtherance and refinement in the work of Roman Jakobson and Emile Benveniste, who with Saussure have had the greatest influence on French poeticians—while it offers a perspective of analysis and an ever-fruitful analogy, does not solve the problems of the poetician. Where, in the field of literary discourse that he wishes to formalize and give laws to, are the equivalents of phonemes, morphemes, even words, clauses, sentences? What are the basic units whose interrelationships define the system? The significant elements from which literary discourse is constructed are far from being clear even to professional literary critics, and in particular there is very little agreement as to what might be called "minimal units," elementary paradigms. Todorov's effort at a synthetic poetics must make use of what he has inherited from the traditions of poetic reflection— particularly studies in genre, also work in metrics, in stylistic "registers," in narrative "point of view," and so forth—which, of diverse provenance, sometimes appear a rather heteroclite assemblage. And he must, while organizing this material, do some invention of his own.

Much of the inherited material that informs Todorov's understanding and exposition of literary discourse comes from the work of the Russian Formalists—dating largely from the 1920s, but only much more recently known in the West—and his command of this work constitutes one of his great strengths as a poetician, indeed perhaps makes him uniquely qualified to undertake a structural poetics. There are in fact direct links of influence connecting Saussurian linguistics, Jakobsonian linguistics, Russian and Prague formalisms; and then, largely through Claude Lévi-Strauss's adaptations of Jakobsonian linguistics within anthropology, between all of these and French structuralism. But Todorov, as one who knows the texts of the Russian and Prague traditions directly, has been able to make detailed and effective use of the work of such pioneer poeticians as Victor Shklovski, Boris Eikhenbaum, Juri Tynianov, Boris Tomachevski, Vladimir Propp, Mikail Bakhtin, Jan Mukarovsky, and Jakobson himself.

One may call these analysts and critics poeticians even though they did not often aspire to a unified theory of literature, since they ever attempted to think about the definition and the components of what they called "literariness"; to use individual works as illustrations of the principles at work in genres, and in literature as a whole; and to isolate (and to name) the elementary units of verbal artifacts. Their constant emphasis on the "constructedness" of literature—its artifactual quality, its fabrication from component "devices" and "motifs"—resulted in work that, whatever the blind alleys and misdirected polemics it may have involved, remains of a rare usefulness to critics interested in the ways in which literature works, most particularly, perhaps, within the field of narrative. Propp—to take just one example—offered in *The Morphology of the Folktale* (1928) a remarkable instance of formalization and progress, in a field previously marked by vast scholarship but little pertinent analysis, by providing the principles of a morphology, that is, a study of the form and structure of the tale, breaking it down into its component parts so that one could both understand how these parts combine to form a complete tale (and to define what "completeness" means), and find a grounds for comparison with other tales, on the basis of a universal structural model in terms of which individual variations become comprehensible. More than any other single source, the Russian Formalist tradition provides Todorov with examples of what it means to decompose literary discourse into its component parts, and to study the logic of the possible significant combinations of parts. The pages of Todorov's *Poetics* that many readers will find most useful—those concerning syntactic elements of texts, and narrative syntax in particular—stand as the best examples of French structuralist rethinking of Russian Formalist positions.

Todorov's *Poetics* is a summary book, in most of its discussions more a program for a poetics than a fully elaborated system. Following the introductory section devoted to the definition of poetics, Todorov considers three principal aspects of texts that any competent reader must, consciously or unconsciously, activate as templates of organization and meaning. The semantic aspect, Todorov notes, appears to be omnipresent in interpretive criticism. Yet such criticism rarely addresses the semantic in the perspective that interests poetics, that is, "the general conditions of the genesis of meaning." Todorov seeks here to understand the kinds of operations that allow signification and symbolization to take place. The second aspect, the verbal, concerns the "manner" of presentation of verbal messages, and covers such questions (analyzed in detail by Gérard Genette, another notable figure in current French literary theory, to whose work Todorov refers here) as mode, time, perspective, voice. Finally, the syntactic aspect concerns textual structures. Here we find the formalist-structuralist concern with minimal textual units and the modes of their combination, the effort to discern basic typologies of plot structure, temporal and spatial ordering: the various questions of textual construction that structuralist poetics has addressed most decisively.

It is no accident that Todorov develops and illustrates his arguments here by a more detailed discussion of narrative syntax, a subject to which he has made major contributions in the wake of the Russian Formalists, and which, partly under his guidance, has become part of what the French now call "narratology." Narrative lends itself particularly well to syntactic analysis since the accomplishment of a narrative action almost of necessity takes the form of the sentence (remember Alice puzzling over "Jabberwocky": *"somebody* killed *something:* that's clear, at any rate"—the syntax at least is clear) and the whole of a narrative may be analogous to a sentence writ large. As Propp discovered in his *Morphology,* the

plots of such formulaic literature as folk tale, at least, can be illumi-
nated by a "functionalist" analysis, where *function* is defined as
"an act of a character, defined from the point of view of its significance for the course of the action" as a whole. Functions are
stable, isolatable elements no matter what character performs them.
They then combine into sequences, which within the genre of the
Russian fairy tale follow a prescribed order. Todorov is able to
generalize and to formalize further such analyses, seeing all narrative as composed of propositions or clauses (the French *proposition* means both), and clauses as minimally composed of a subject
or "actant"—like a proper name, semantically void until predicated
—and a predicate of various sorts. He can then go on to show how
clauses combine in sequences, where a sequence may be defined
(following Tomachevski) as what moves us from one state or situation to another; and then (developing the suggestions of Shklovski) how sequences can be ordered—by embedding, enchaining,
alternation—to create a more complex narrative.

As Todorov suggests in his pages on "specifications and reactions," this basic model is susceptible of considerable refinement
and elaboration from further distinctions that can be derived logically from the categories of syntax, that is, by study of the model
itself as it generates insights into the behavior of narrative. Here it
is that the linguistic model of structuralism may show itself the
most suggestive, though we may not yet be in a position to say
whether it will provide a quasi-scientific basis to future studies in
narrative—a set of precise categories allowing comparative analyses
—or rather a richly instructive metaphor whose main value may
come, not from analytic precision, but from the way it helps us
think about the nature of narrative.

In the remainder of *Poetics*, Todorov takes up the question of
literary history, which one might think of as a diachronic poetics.
Here we find a particular concern for genres and their variations
through time. The concept of genre has in fact assumed new importance in contemporary poetics, not as the prescriptive set of
rules it has sometimes been considered in the past (e.g., the
"rules" of neoclassical tragedy) but as a set of norms and expecta-
tions that structure our reading of texts, allowing us to organize
sense-making according to conventional patterns, and to perceive

variations in the use of convention. Finally, Todorov ends by facing the possibility that poetics cannot be an autonomous science because its object, literature, is not itself autonomous, but a special case of human discourse and symbolization. The "literariness" that is the object of poetics is only relative: if at one level of analysis we can speak of what distinguishes literary from nonliterary uses of language, at another we need to consider both as a continuum. Hence poetics, as the study of literary discourse, may be only a transitional science that will need to be supplanted by a general science of discourses.

There has in fact been a natural evolution of structuralism in its literary applications toward semiotics, or the general theory of signs: a more universalistic science than poetics, and one that promises to show how literary discourse interlocks with other linguistic and social codes. Yet semiotics, while it informs structuralist thinking about literature insofar as this is concerned with the behavior of signs and the production of meaning—structuralism and semiotics here become indistinguishable—ought not to engulf or devour poetics, which will remain necessary as a specific discipline and field of inquiry so long as literature is considered a human endeavor and social institution somehow distinct from everyday uses of language. So long as we continue to want to confer on literature some measure of closure and interrelationship—however tentative and even arbitrary—poetics will seem necessary.

It seems necessary, too, to stress the importance of the kind of poetics Todorov has attempted to sketch in this volume, whatever its admitted gaps and limitations, when we note the rapidity with which in recent years literary critics have, rather too glibly, announced the movement beyond structuralism, into various forms of "post-structuralism," of which the "deconstruction" of Jacques Derrida has received the greatest attention in this country. Structuralism tends to present a static conception of its field of analysis, which may be a necessary function of its effort to formalize its subject of study, with the result that its principles and categories—in the study of narrative, for instance—often appear inadequate to account for the dynamics of texts, and the temporality of reading. The structuralist preoccupation with minimal units and paradigms gives little account of the transformatory role of human fictions, where language, inhabited by desire, intends as much as it signifies. It has of course been notoriously a reproach addressed to structuralism that it brackets history, giving no clue to the dynamics of historical change. Literary criticism of post-structuralist persuasions has found itself haunted anew by such thinkers as Hegel, Marx, Nietzsche, and Freud, all of whom were centrally concerned with change and its motors, with the dynamics of social and psychic transformation and the participation of language, and the imaginary, in the interpretation and constitution of the notion of the human. There have been various moves to unlock and break out of what have been seen as the constricting forms and patternings of structuralism. The work of Derrida, and the last books of Barthes, for example, have foregrounded notions of play, the decentering of structures, force as opposed to form, and the radical uncertainty of language itself.

To the extent that post-structuralism has been a French phenomenon, it has taken place in a context where the contributions of structuralist thought were already accepted as solid achievements, which could then be used, taken apart, opened up, in the movement beyond, whereas the current popularity of some forms of post-structuralism in this country seems at times to be without context, indeed simply the indulgence, under a new guise, of the traditional American penchant for exegesis and interpretation. Relatively few American critics appear to have absorbed the lessons of a structuralist poetics. Some of them have simply performed a shortcut back to interpretation, now flying post-structuralist banners. To recognize this is to argue for the importance of an endeavor such as Todorov's in *Poetics*.

Part of the reaction against structuralism has of course been caused by the shortcuts practiced by critics calling themselves structuralists who offered abusive applications of its lessons. The linguistic model too easily became a facile metaphor. Saussure's doctrines were applied directly to the analysis of texts without any questioning, on the critic's part, of their pertinence. The notion of the "arbitrariness of the sign"—by which Saussure meant the conventional, unmotivated choice of a certain acoustic image to signify a certain concept—has, for instance, been directly applied in wildly metaphorical ways to textual readings. What has often gone unexamined is the logic that should guide extrapolation from model to practice. As Jonathan Culler persuasively argues in *Structuralist Poetics* (Cornell University Press, 1975), the linguistic model does not in and of itself constitute a "discovery procedure" that will automatically lead you to the pertinent features of a text: you must identify what needs explanation before reference to the model will help you. The linguistic model is not hermeneutic, it does not offer a tool for interpretation, but rather a grounds for organizing the interpretable and the results of interpretation. The misuses of structuralist thought in literary criticism most often appear as a failure to understand the importance of poetics as the necessary intermediate ground between linguistics and interpretation.

Todorov has himself written a number of essays in applied criticism, especially essays in what he has called (in *The Poetics of Prose*) the "specification of theory," attempting to test and to refine general theory in interaction with a text, a body of texts, a genre. But he does not lose sight of the distinction between interpretation and theory, and the necessity to consider the procedures of the interpreter in the context of a coherent poetics. His essays in criticism refer us from the specific instance to the general category it illustrates, and from meaning to the conditions of meaning, seeing the individual work as part of a class of works, and this, in turn, as part of the larger network of signifying processes. Poetics is consistently the point of reference of his work, and he has with exemplary clarity maintained and pursued his understanding that the pertinence of structuralist thinking to the study of literature is in pure, not applied, criticism. And in providing the elements of a poetics, however heterogenous and incomplete they may be, he has forcefully shown the necessary place of structural poetics within our contemporary literary theorizing and interpretation. If after the heady days of the initial impact of structuralism, when the claims to foundation of a science of literature were regularly announced with totalistic solemnity, there has come a perceptible reaction, one must argue that within the limits it sets for itself, a poetics such as that Todorov proposes remains indispensable to those seriously concerned with literature.

Northrop Frye, in the course of his polemic on the state of

literary criticism, dreams of a textbook "expounding its fundamental principles." It is clear that any contemporary textbook for
the study of literature would have to include many of the issues
addressed by Todorov. While Todorov has not himself provided
such a textbook, his *Poetics* is both a primer and prolegomenon,
introducing its reader to a field of knowledge and mapping the
work yet to be done. Todorov is naturally and unfailingly a peda-
gogue, concerned to make his and others' discoveries available in
the clearest, most comprehensible formulations, and to lead his
reader to progressive mastery of the field. One always senses in
Todorov's work the desire to be useful, which has made him—in
a Parisian literary scene that often appears to value the striking,
the paradoxical, and the abstruse more than the useful—an un-
usually reliable figure in critical theory. At the close of the new
preface he has written for this translation, where he describes his
current work-in-progress, one detects both an enlargement of hori-
zons in his research—which appears to be becoming more "anthro-
pological" in concern—and the continuing commitment to a discourse on literature which is in the best sense didactic, which
eschews exercises in personal interpretation in favor of communi-
cable knowledge of literature. "Knowledge of" literature, we suggested earlier, is not to be confused with "information about"
literature, which, however necessary at times, is another discourse
that merely situates the literary discourse. Knowledge of literature,
in Todorov's acceptation, rather means a constant scrutiny of that
which makes literary discourse possible, the system of meaning it
uses and creates, as part of the vast project of human sense-making
in sign systems. The reader according to Todorov—and Todorov
himself as reader—reads ever with an awareness of the larger system to which the text at hand refers, which it actualizes in the
creation of its own "new word."

Preface to the English Edition
Poetics, Past and Future

One day a friend who teaches in an American university took me to task: "I was using your book on poetics in my course and quoted something the students claimed they couldn't find in their copies—and they were right: the two editions of your text are so different!"

The first version was written in 1967 as part of a collective volume called *What Is Structuralism?* The second, intended for publication as a separate book, dates from 1973. Between the first occasion and the second, a considerable renewal of poetics had occurred in France, and I felt obliged to take it into account. I too had changed, in ways not exactly opposed to, but at any rate different from the general case: whereas poetics might be said to have "triumphed" (though only in a manner of speaking, of course; in France, poetics has never known an institutional triumph), I myself felt less and less ready to assume a triumphant language. All of which I explained to my friend, who replied: "In other words you'll be rewriting this book every six or seven years!"

The present translation affords me an opportunity to make his prediction come true. But this time I have decided upon a different solution: that of leaving the text intact and writing a preface. A solution open to criticism, of course: an attentive reader would already have had no difficulty discovering discrepancies or even contradictions between the portions remaining from the 1967 version and those added in 1973; such discrepancies would now be exacerbated by adding a 1980 stratum to the other two, a stratum necessarily somewhat different from them (if I had not altered my way of looking at things, why add a preface?). Certainly the 1967 version was, in itself, more coherent; but was it also more accurate? Yet if I decline, for the moment, to rewrite the whole book, I do so less out of indolence than because of the different way in which I now perceive the relation between history and science (or truth). Obliged to reread my text, I experience it as somehow external to me, as if someone else had written it (I intend no value judgment here). This someone else is historically situated; if I were to rewrite the book, I would do so to erase such signs of time, to reorient my enterprise from history to science; yet that would be an illusion: I should have merely replaced the signs of the past by those of the present, yielding to the stupendous egocentric mirage wherein zero equals infinity: the present is eternity. That is why I have decided to complete the original text, which describes a certain state of poetics, by two remarks of historical character: one on the past of poetics (of literary theory), the other on its future; in doing so, my way of seeing things today may also become evident.

Discourse about literature is born with literature itself; we find the earliest specimens in certain fragments of the Vedas or in Homer. This can be no accident: though it is difficult to agree about the exact identity of "literature," it is certain that this name, or one of its equivalents, has always been used to designate an utterance that must provoke the pleasure or the interest of its hearers and readers, that is intended to last, and that is thereby more highly elaborated than everyday speech. Hence an awareness of language is fundamental to the literary act, and even if the writer is not tempted by abstract reflection, literature itself has always had a metaliterary dimension.

From its inception, this discourse is not *one*, with regard to its finality and its forms, but takes two different directions: these are exegesis and theory. In the first case, the goal will be to elucidate or to make explicit or to interpret a certain work: the *Iliad*, the Bible, the sacred hymns. Things are much less simple on the side where, instead of this object that history serves up already defined and about whose identity there is no doubt, we find an object constructed by the very discourse that describes it. When the theme of such reflection is allegory, or narrative, or catharsis, these units are not given in advance (unless by some previous theoretical discourse), and the fact that in order to illustrate such concepts we always refer to the same works (the *Iliad*, the Bible) does not change matters at all: the same empirical object has an infinite number of properties, and each theoretician can—in theory!—select those that suit him, leaving the rest aside. Theoretical discourse about literature does not bear upon works but, precisely, upon "literature" or upon other general categories of the empirical objects intuitively compared. It is this possibility of choice—and therefore, ultimately, this threat of arbitrariness—that produces the fundamental problem of literary theory.

These two discourses about literature have sustained, down through the centuries, highly variable (and often inimical) relations; but actually they can never do without each other. Exegesis always presupposes a theory (however unconscious), for it needs descriptive concepts, or more simply a vocabulary, in order to refer to the work studied; now, definitions of concepts are precisely what constitute theory. But theory also presupposes the existence of exegesis, for it is by means of exegesis that theory makes contact with the substance that serves as its point of departure: literary discourse itself. Each of the two can correct the other: the theoretician criticizes the exegete's discourse, and the exegete in his turn shows the inadequacies of theory in relation to the object studied, the works.

The historical fate of the two discourses about literature, exegesis and theory, will be quite different (though both will be sustained in every period), and this difference can be read as a consequence of how each constitutes its object. Exegetic discourse has from its inception taken two separate paths: on the one hand, *literal exegesis*, which consists in elucidating the meaning of such and such an incomprehensible word, in supplying the references for such and such an allusion, in explicating such and such a syntactical construction; on the other hand, *allegorical exegesis*, which seeks a different meaning for a text (or for a segment of text) already possessing one. Despite the ideological transformations of the contents involved, transformations that have occurred in the course of centuries, and despite the change in the formulation of the rules to be followed in both instances, exegetic discourse remains remarkably stable, and these two paths are still followed, merely taking different forms: today, for instance, those of philology and criticism. The object of literary theory, on the other hand, changes radically from one period to the next, to the point where we risk committing an anachronism by using the expression "literary theory" to designate certain discourses of the past that, if they are incontestably theoretical, have not defined their object as being "literature." The unity of this object derives solely from what nineteenth- and twentieth-century Europeans call by the same name, *literature,* the works that these theories take as their point of departure or their illustrations. Literary theory itself has a unity only in a certain perspective, whereas its historical evolution unfolds with many interruptions.

Aristotle's *Poetics,* twenty-five hundred years old, is at once the first work entirely devoted to "literary theory" (quotation marks are indispensable here to forestall anachronism) and one of the most important in the canon. The simultaneous presence of these two features is not without paradox: it is as if a man with an already graying moustache were to emerge from his mother's womb (though obviously the comparison is a misleading one). We can offer scarcely any similar example—perhaps Pannini's *Grammar,* at once the firstborn and the masterpiece of linguistics (yet this text plays only a minor part in the history of knowledge), or, closer to us, the same Aristotle's *Logic.*

The object of the *Poetics* is not literature (or what we call literature), and in this sense the book is not a work of literary theory, but of representation (*mimesis*) utilizing language. Consequently, after an introduction devoted to representation in general, Aristotle describes the properties of the representative (or fictional) genres, i.e., epic and drama, which are analyzed on a series of levels, on the one hand, and of segments, on the other (actually only one kind of drama, tragedy, is dealt with, the part on comedy being lost or simply nonexistent). Furthermore, the *Poetics* gives no consideration to poetry (which certainly existed at the time), though we know that poetry will be considered, in the modern period, as the purest incarnation of literature.

In the next twenty centuries, literature will continue to constitute the object of various theoretical discourses, even if these are not exclusively "theories of literature." Among these discourses, we must first mention *rhetoric:* certain aspects of literature are to be found here, in a sense taken over completely. Originally the object of rhetoric was public discourse (that of the orator, that of the lawyer); but, since all aspects of discourse must be described, those that public discourse shares with literature are also touched on: notably in the case of style ("elocution"). Moreover, as public discourse loses a great deal of its importance following the disappearance of the early democracies, literature will occupy an ever-growing place in subsequent rhetorics, until it becomes, after the Renaissance, the unique source of examples cited by rhetoricians. Another well-instituted discourse that covers certain aspects of literature is that of *hermeneutics,* or theory of interpretation. The object around which hermeneutics developed consists of sacred texts; but once again, certain verbal structures are discussed that are just as likely to be found in profane writings: thus the medieval hermeneuts do not neglect poetic allegory. Something of the same thing occurs in the case of the other great civilizations in which there exists a "literary theory": Indian, Arabic, or Chinese works of poetics discuss semantic or psychological problems that transcend mere literature (though without "covering" it), and integrate it into groupings of variable contours.

Things begin to change somewhat with the Renaissance, in several regards. First of all, Aristotle's *Poetics* is exhumed and made to play a role comparable to that of holy writ: works of poetics will now be nothing more, so to speak, than commentaries on the *Poetics!* But in truth this book is rather betrayed by its glory, which functions as no more than a screen between itself and its readers: the text is so celebrated that no one dares contest or even, finally, read it at all. Instead it is reduced to a few formulas quickly transformed into clichés that, removed from their context, betray their author's thought altogether.

In the second place, reflection concerning genres is intensified. Such reflection has a tradition as old as "literary theory" in general, since, as we have seen, Aristotle's *Poetics* had already described the specific properties of epic and tragedy. And the same path has been followed ever since, in works of extremely various natures. But it is particularly since the Renaissance that this type of study has established its own traditions: texts succeed each other on the "rules" of tragedy and comedy, of epic and romance, of the various lyric genres. The prosperity of such discourse is certainly linked to the dominant ideological structures and to the very notion of genre that each period arrives at—which is to say, that of a norm not to be violated. Genres certainly belong to literature (or to "poetry," or to "belles-lettres") but are a unit on a lower level, obtained by decomposition of the primary one, comparable in this sense to the objects of earlier "literary theory," and yet different as well: whereas symbol, or representation, or figurative style are abstract properties of literary discourse (whose extension is consequently greater than mere literature), genres result from another type of analysis, that of literature into its parts.

And finally, the notion of the unity of the arts begins to spread, generating a theory of the arts that seeks to link at least the two most reputed practices, poetry and painting. This theory is transformed in the eighteenth century into a discipline, aesthetics, in which room will be allowed for literary theory, at least insofar as literary theory can be integrated into a general theory of the arts. Lessing and Kant are the first great wielders of this discourse, but their work is anticipated by a long series of investigations, from Leonardo da Vinci down to Shaftesbury.

None of these three developments leads directly to the constitution of "literature" as a unit, yet all herald it: already we possess the superior category, art (whose subdivision according to media will be easy enough), as well as entities of lower rank, genres; we are also furnished with a reference text, the *Poetics*, which guarantees the continuity of the tradition.

It is with the advent of (German) romanticism that the notion of literature is established in its autonomy, and this is also the beginning of literary theory in the strict sense (without quotation marks). The concepts of representation and imitation no longer play a dominant role, being replaced at the summit of the hierarchy by the concept of the beautiful, and those related to it: the absence of external finality, the harmonious coherence among the parts of the whole, the untranslatable character of the work of art. All these notions point toward the autonomy of literature and of its works, and lead to an inquiry into their specific properties. It is indeed this inquiry that we find in the romantic texts. But their influence is not immediate, especially on institutional literary studies, doubtless a consequence of the form these texts assume: either they are fragments that in many respects participate in poetry itself (as in the case of Friedrich Schlegel and Novalis), or else they are systematic philosophical treatises that continue the tradition of aesthetics, where literature occupies a very limited place (as is the case with Schelling and Hegel).

Academic literary theory is born, then, only with the twentieth century, in several countries, one after the other. In the first two decades of this century, the country of renewal is Russia, where a current of ideas known as Formalism is constituted. Between the wars the center of gravity shifts to Germany; literary theory then divides into several tendencies, some linked to stylistics, others to a "morphological" approach. In the thirties and forties, various currents of formal criticism and literary theory develop in England and the United States, of which the most celebrated is the so-called New Criticism. All these groups have their common point of departure in romantic aesthetics, which leads them to assert the autonomy of literature and consequently of its theory; but unlike the romantics, these theoreticians concern themselves with an analysis of the literary work, thereby linking up with the Aristotelian tradition which, it will be remembered, was concerned to distinguish the pertinent levels and segments of works. The various formalists of the twentieth century are therefore closer to the spirit of the *Poetics* than were its sixteenth-century admirers, since in a sense they resume the undertaking at the same point where Aristotle left off; thereby they achieve a happy synthesis of the various tendencies that had hitherto dominated "literary theory," and they lead to the establishment of our modern discipline.

Among the major European countries, it is in France that literary theory appears most belatedly. Perhaps because of the slow start it assumed in comparison to other countries, philology continues particularly active in France to the middle of the twentieth century; and when it comes to be contested, it is not in the name of a theoretical reflection, but on the basis of other critical methods based on various tendencies of modern ideology: Marxist criticism, psychoanalytical criticism, phenomenological criticism. If we want to find a theory of literature in France during the last hundred and fifty years, we must turn to the writings of the poets and novelists. From Flaubert and Mallarmé to Valéry, it is writers who play a part comparable to the role of the German romantics; the content of such a doctrine, moreover, remains the same, at least in its general contours. But, again, their source as well as their forms of expression keep these ideas from crossing the academic threshold, and they remain in a state of abstract formulas rather than being embodied in an analytic and descriptive effort.

Matters begin to change appreciably only after the Second World War; again we must distinguish two periods, one lasting till the early sixties, the second continuing since then. During the first are elaborated several major works of reflection on literature in general, though these still come from writers rather than from scholars, and the systematic description of the literary work remains in the background. Thus Sartre proposes (notably in *What Is Literature?*, 1948) a theory of literature we might call sociological, though it does not lack all concern for formal analysis: it is the relation between the text and the public for which it is written that is given pride of place here. Maurice Blanchot's inquiries (*L'Espace littéraire*, 1955; *Le Livre à venir*, 1959) have a more philosophical character: Blanchot seeks to grasp the necessarily fugitive site where all literature originates, the metaphysical choice that leads the writer to produce his first line. Despite their authors' genius— or perhaps because of it—these two inquiries have not really formed any kind of school (though they have not been without influence): their ideas may have seemed too dependent on the expression that sustains them to lend themselves to academic extrapolation. In the same period appear several other works of literary theory in the modern sense, i.e., which describe certain properties of literary texts. Hence a study is made of point of view in the novel and the relations sustained between narrator and character (J. Pouillon, *Temps et roman*, 1946); or else of the roles assumed by the characters in a dramatic universe, and the types of situation in which they may find themselves (E. Souriau, *Les deux cents mille situations dramatiques,* 1947). But again these are no more than isolated phenomena.

The situation of literary theory really changes only in the sixties, and the decisive factor of this change is the influence of structuralist methodology on all the human sciences. Under the leadership of Lévi-Strauss, the structuralist strategy, elaborated in linguistics and transposed by him to ethnology, acquires great prestige and affects extremely varied fields of knowledge. Now structuralism invariably favors theoretical discourse; in literary studies too it favors theory at the expense of exegesis. Its influence will be all the greater in that the ideological bases of structuralism are the very ones that romantic aesthetics had elaborated and that had remained familiar to literary scholars in the reflections of the post-romantic writers. This influence also determines the form literary theory gives its object: this will be *literary discourse,* i.e., the totality of verbal structures that function within each work.

History is always much more fragile and conjectural than we suppose, since the point of view taken makes us select certain phenomena as pertinent and reject others as not; this fragility intensifies as we approach the present, since the "judgment of time" can no longer come to our assistance. As for the future, we can no longer be dealing with history, of course, but, according to cases, with divination, prophecy, speculation. But I can benefit here from the distance that separates 1980 from 1973 (or from 1967); the future I speak of is a future in relation to the text that follows; for me today it is the present.

If I try to get past the disputes of vocabulary, the personal divergences involved, I can distinguish four main directions followed by present-day literary studies:

1. The theory of literary discourse is being integrated into a general theory of discourses. We shall find the reasons for this change in the present work, and notably in the concluding chapter; they mainly concern the fact that literary specificity is not of a linguistic (and hence universal) nature, but historical and cultural.

This new discipline, which has *discourses* for its object, is being constituted today in various countries and under different names; distinct from linguistics in that it does not describe language and grammatical mechanisms, but also from poetics in that it does not confine itself to literary discourse, this new discipline bears names like *pragmatics, rhetoric* (a *new* rhetoric, of course), *textual linguistics, translinguistics,* and doubtless others as well. Many problems broached in the following pages are investigated—though how much more learnedly!—in this new context, exclusive of any literary reference. The signs of this development are increasing today, and come from all directions: from that of the linguists concerned with units beyond the sentence; from that of the social scientists concerned with the verbal properties of discourses responsible for collective representations; from literary men themselves, finally, who include in their inquiries certain nonliterary texts. To cite but one example, what a difference between *Anatomy of Criticism* (1957), based on an inquiry into literary specificity, and the more recent texts of Northrop Frye, whose object is, increasingly, verbal culture as a whole (and not just literature).

2. What I called, above, literal exegesis (or philology) forms a second major direction of work (even if such appellations seem anachronistic to its partisans). The question of critical pluralism often strikes me as poorly phrased because of the lack of distinction between what used to be called literal exegesis and allegorical exegesis; to refer to more recent authors, I might, with Bakhtin, identify *precision* and *depth* as exegetic ideals corresponding to different phases of critical reading. As was customary to say, at least since Spinoza (if not since Origen), literal exegesis has two wings, one linguistic and the other historical. Linguistic analysis (in the broad sense, including stylistics, or "pragmatics," etc.) distinguishes the true from the false: whatever the critical point of view, it is admitted that the subjects of sentences in the prose of the later Henry James are by preference abstract nouns; that this writer favors intransitive verbs or negation; the pluralist has nothing to say on this matter. The same is true of historical analysis, even if matters are here more complex: a certain aesthetic theory, a certain ideological discourse did or did not exist at a certain time, there is no third solution; a discourse acquires its

meaning only within a particular context, and it is incontestable that a better knowledge of this context is pertinent to the comprehension of the discourse. It is because both wings function properly that we have that feeling of a perfectly mastered flight, as upon reading such masterpieces of literal exegesis as the recent works of Joseph Frank on Dostoevsky or of Ian Watt on Conrad (which are merely cited as examples).

3. The question of pluralism becomes pertinent once more, on the other hand, in dealing with what was once called allegorical exegesis (and what we call, quite simply, criticism). But we immediately risk, upon separating literal and allegorical exegesis, falling into a Lanson's crude and myopic disdain for critics. Nothing would be more erroneous (or, more modestly, more remote from what I believe to be correct). Every work is rewritten by its reader, who imposes upon it a new grid of interpretation for which he is not generally responsible but which comes to him from his culture, from his time, in short from another discourse; all comprehension is the encounter of two discourses: a dialogue. It is futile and silly to try to leave off being oneself in order to become someone else; were one to succeed, the result would be of no interest (since it would be a pure reproduction of the initial discourse). By its very existence, the science of ethnology proves to us, if need be, that we *gain* by being different from what we seek to understand. This interpretation (in the necessary double sense of translation and comprehension) is the condition of survival of the antecedent text; but no less so, I should say, of contemporary discourse. Hence interpretation is no longer true or false but rich or poor, revealing or sterile, stimulating or dull.

If Roland Barthes (that unforgettable master who taught me to renounce both masters and mastery) reads a text, he tells us what our modern sensibility finds in it; it is an encounter between Racine and Barthes, Sade and Barthes, Balzac and Barthes (it is not the individuals, of course, who are concerned).

4. The final direction is that of historical poetics (of literary history, strictly speaking). History cannot have as its object the separate works themselves, but only what transcends them: the categories of literary discourse and their more or less stable

combinations, for which we possess a traditional name: genres. Here we accept a degree of generality somewhere between the universalism of the theory of discourses and the particularism of exegesis; and we resort to formal analysis as much as to ideological analysis, for genre is as closely related to linguistic forms as it is to the history of ideas. This direction especially characterizes the study of literary discourse: when we make a theory of conversation, we take as an example any conversation that may be available, or we invent one; what is essential is that we all agree to recognize it as a possible conversation. But of all the literary "possibles," only certain ones are realized, and these are the only ones that interest us; literary studies have as their object a corpus and not a discursive competence, for literature has existed in history (this perspective is to be added to the "rhetorical" or "pragmatic" point of view without cancelling it). And we are "doing" history when, again like Ian Watt, we study the rise of the novel at the dawn of capitalism, or the transformation of the great European myths following the romantic crisis; or when, like Bakhtin, we try to describe the different conceptions of time and space functioning in this or that kind of prose narrative, from Antiquity to the Renaissance.

Have I myself a place among these major directions? I am presently studying texts that concern the discovery and conquest of America; to do so, I rely on a certain conception of what a discourse is and of how its meaning appears; I therefore take advantage of the general theory of discourses. In my reading, I try to be precise: I am attentive to style and to discursive forms, and I read as many related texts as possible to steep myself in the ideology of the period: I perform literal exegesis. But my project is historical: I am concerned with the development of the site we have reserved for the *other* since the Renaissance; and the sixteenth-century texts, already highly discrepant among themselves, reveal an image structured very differently from the way it will appear in the eighteenth century (or in the twentieth century). And beyond this, I am trying to speak to my contemporaries (what the Church fathers called the moral, or tropological, meaning) about questions that touch us all: about tolerance and xenophobia, about colonialism and communication, about assimilation of the other and identification with the other, about hidden or apparent feelings of superiority; this is my allegorical exegesis. My work therefore participates in each of these directions (should I say that I am hunting four hares at once?), which seems to me, moreover, the rule and not the exception; to distinguish them is no less justified, and even necessary.

And poetics, in all this? Poetics is recognizable in each of these directions of inquiry, even if we do not always feel the need to name it. It is in transformation, and that is the best sign of its vitality.

T.T.   May 1980

Introduction to Poetics

Chapter One
Definition of Poetics

To understand what poetics is, we must start from a general and of course a somewhat simplified image of literary studies. It is unnecessary to describe actual schools and tendencies; it will suffice to recall the positions taken with regard to several basic choices.

Initially there are two attitudes to be distinguished: one sees the literary text itself as a sufficient object of knowledge; the other considers each individual text as the manifestation of an abstract structure. (I herewith disregard biographical studies, which are not literary, as well as journalistic writings, which are not "studies.") These two options are not, as we shall see, incompatible; we can even say that they achieve a necessary complementarity; nonetheless, depending on whether we emphasize one or the other, we can clearly distinguish between the two tendencies.

Let us begin with a few words about the first attitude, for which the literary work is the ultimate and unique object, and which we shall here and henceforth call *interpretation*. Interpretation, which is sometimes also called *exegesis, commentary, explication de texte, close reading, analysis,* or even just *criticism* (such a list does not mean we cannot distinguish or even set in opposition

3

some of these terms), is defined, in the sense we give it here, by its aim, which is *to name the meaning of the text examined.* This aim forthwith determines the ideal of this attitude—which is to make the text itself speak; i.e., it is a fidelity to the object, to the *other,* and consequently an effacement of the subject—as well as its drama, which is to be forever incapable of realizing *the* meaning, but only *a* meaning, subject to historical and psychological contingencies. This ideal, this drama will be modulated down through the history of commentary, itself coextensive with the history of humanity.

In effect, it is impossible to interpret a work, literary or otherwise, for and in itself, without leaving it for a moment, without projecting it elsewhere than upon itself. Or rather, this task is possible, but then description is merely a word-for-word repetition of the work itself. It espouses the forms of the work so closely that the two are identical. And, in a certain sense, every work constitutes its own best description.

What comes closest to this ideal but invisible description is, simply, a reading, insofar as a reading is no more than a manifestation of the work. Yet the process of reading is already not without consequences: two readings of a book are never identical. In reading, we trace a passive writing; we add and suppress, in the text read, what we want or do not want to find there; reading is no longer immanent, once there is a reader.

What are we to say, then, of that active and no longer passive writing that is criticism, whether of scientific or artistic inspiration? How can we write a text while remaining faithful to another text, keeping it intact? How can we articulate a discourse that is immanent to another discourse? By the fact that there is writing and no longer only reading, the critic says something that the work studied does not say, even if he claims to say the same thing. By the fact that he writes a new book, the critic suppresses the one he is talking about.

Which is not to say that there are not degrees in this transgression of immanence.

One of the dreams of positivism in the human sciences is the distinction, even the opposition, between interpretation—subjective, vulnerable, ultimately arbitrary—and description, a certain and definitive activity. Since the nineteenth century, projects have been formulated—projects for a "scientific criticism" that, having banished all "interpretation," would be nothing but pure "description" of works. No sooner did such "definitive descriptions" appear than the public eagerly forgot them, as if they differed in no way from the earlier criticism; and the public was not mistaken. The phenomena of signification, which constitute the object of interpretation, do not lend themselves to "description," if we want to assign this word a meaning both absolute and objective. Hence in literary studies: what can be objectively "described"—the number of words, or of syllables, or of sounds—does not permit us to deduce the meaning; and reciprocally, where meaning is to be determined, material measurement is of little use.

But to say "everything is interpretation" does not signify "all interpretations are equivalent." Reading is a trajectory in the space of the text; a trajectory not limited to the succession of letters, from left to right and from top to bottom (that is the *only* unique trajectory, which explains why the text has no unique meaning), but one that separates the contiguous and juxtaposes the remote, one that in fact constitutes the text in space and not in linearity. The famous "hermeneutic circle," which postulates the necessary copresence of the whole and its parts and thereby makes impossible an absolute beginning, already testifies to the necessary plurality of interpretations. But all "circles" are not equally valid: they allow us to pass through more or fewer points of the textual space, they compel us to omit a greater or lesser number of its elements. And we all know in practice that some readings are more faithful than others—even if none is entirely so. The difference between interpretation and description (of meaning) is one of degree, not of nature; but it is no less useful in a didactic perspective.

If *interpretation* was the generic term for the first type of analysis to which we submit the literary text, the second attitude remarked above can be inscribed within the general context of *science*. By using this word, which the "average literary man" does not favor, we intend to refer less to the degree of precision this activity achieves (a precision necessarily relative) than to the general perspective chosen by the analyst: his goal is no longer the description of the particular work, the designation of its meaning, but the establishment of general laws of which this particular text is the product.

Within this second attitude, we may distinguish several varieties, at first glance very remote from one another. Indeed, we find here, side by side, psychological or psychoanalytic, sociological or ethnological studies, as well as those derived from philosophy or from the history of ideas. All deny the autonomous character of the literary work and regard it as the manifestation of laws that are external to it and that concern the psyche, or society, or even the "human mind." The object of such studies is to transpose the work into the realm considered fundamental: it is a labor of decipherment and translation; the literary work is the expression of "something," and the goal of such studies is to reach this "something" through the poetic code. Depending on whether the nature of this object to be reached is philosophical, psychological, sociological, or something else, the study in question will be inscribed within one of these types of discourse (one of these "sciences"), each of which possesses, of course, many subdivisions. Such an activity is related to science insofar as its object is no longer the particular phenomenon but the (psychological, sociological, etc.) law that the phenomenon illustrates.

Poetics breaks down the symmetry thus established between interpretation and science in the field of literary studies. In contradistinction to the interpretation of particular works, it does not seek to name meaning, but aims at a knowledge of the general laws that preside over the birth of each work. But in contradistinction to such sciences as psychology, sociology, etc., it seeks these laws within literature itself. Poetics is therefore an approach to literature at once "abstract" and "internal."

It is not the literary work itself that is the object of poetics: what poetics questions are the properties of that particular discourse that is literary discourse. Each work is therefore regarded only as the manifestation of an abstract and general structure, of which it is but one of the possible realizations. Whereby this science is no longer concerned with actual literature, but with a possible literature in other words, with that abstract property that constitutes the singularity of the literary phenomenon: *literariness.* The goal of this study is no longer to articulate a paraphrase, a descriptive résumé of the concrete work, but to propose a theory of the structure and functioning of literary discourse, a theory that affords a list of literary possibilities, so that existing literary works appear as achieved particular cases. The work will then be projected upon something other than itself, as in the case of psychological or sociological criticism; this *something other* will no longer be a heterogeneous structure, however, but the structure of literary discourse itself. The particular text will be only an instance that allows us to describe the properties of literature.

Is the term "poetics" the right one for this notion? We know that its meaning has varied down through history; but by relying as much on an old tradition as on several recent examples, however isolated, we may employ it without fear. Valéry, who already asserted the necessity of such an activity, had given it the same name: "The name of *Poetics* seems appropriate to such a study if we take the word in its etymological sense, that is, as a name for everything that bears on the creation or composition of works having language at once as their substance and as their instrument —and not in the restricted sense of a collection of aesthetic rules or precepts relating to poetry" (p. 86).

Now let us return to the relation between poetics and the other approaches to the literary work we have just referred to.

The relation between poetics and interpretation is one of complementarity par excellence. A theoretical reflection upon poetics that is not sustained by observations of existing works always turns out to be sterile and invalid. Friedrich Schlegel, in his time, had established an illuminating parallel."Hermeneutics corresponds to grammar as criticism to poetics." This situation is familiar to the linguists, and Benveniste rightly asserts that "reflection on language is fruitful only if it deals first of all with real languages." Interpretation both precedes and follows poetics: the notions of poetics are produced according to the necessities of concrete analysis, which in its turn may advance only by using the instruments elaborated by doctrine. Neither of the two activities takes precedence over the other: both are "secondary." This intimate interpenetration, which often makes the work of criticism an incessant oscillation between poetics and interpretation, must not keep us from distinguishing, in the abstract, the goals of the one attitude from those of the other.

On the other hand, between poetics and the other sciences that may take the literary work for their object, the relation is (at first glance at least) one of incompatibility—to the great regret, it is true, of the eclectics, so numerous among the literati: they are inclined to admit, with equal willingness, an analysis of literature based on linguistics, then another based on psychoanalysis, then a third, based on sociology, then a fourth, based on the history of ideas. . . . The unity of all these procedures is constituted, we are told, by their unique object: literature. But such an assertion is contrary to the elementary principles of scientific research. The unity of science is not constituted by the uniqueness of its object: there is not a "science of bodies," though the bodies are a unique object, but a physics, a chemistry, a geometry. And no one seeks to give equal rights in a "science of bodies" to a "chemical analysis," a "physical analysis," and a "geometrical analysis." It is hardly necessary to repeat that the method creates the object, that the object of a science is not given in nature but represents the result of an elaboration. Freud analyzed several literary works, yet his analyses belong not to the "science of literature" but to psychoanalysis. The other human sciences may make use of literature as a substance for these analyses, but if the latter are good, they belong to the science in question and not to a scattered literary commentary. And if the psychological or sociological analysis of a text is not judged worthy of belonging to psychology or to sociology, it is hard to see why it should be welcomed automatically as a constituent part of the "science of literature."

The notion of a scientific reflection on literature immediately arouses so much mistrust that it is necessary, before dealing with

the problems of poetics, to review some of the arguments raised
against this reflection itself. By becoming aware of these arguments, poetics may be able to avoid more readily the dangers it
is said to incur.

Each of these arguments has been proposed many times over;
hence we must select among the various formulations. Here is a
page from Henry James's famous essay *The Art of Fiction:*

> Nothing . . . is more possible than that [the novelist] be of a turn of
> mind for which this odd, literal opposition of description and dialogue, inci-
> dent and description, has little meaning and light. People often talk of these
> things as if they had a kind of internecine distinctness, instead of melting
> into each other at every breath, and being intimately associated parts of one
> general effort of expression. I cannot imagine composition existing in a series
> of blocks, nor conceive, in any novel worth discussing at all, of a passage of
> description that is not in its intention narrative, a passage of dialogue that is
> not in its intention descriptive, a touch of truth of any sort that does not
> partake of the nature of incident, or an incident that derives its interest from
> any other source than the general and only source of the success of a work of
> art—that of being illustrative. A novel is a living thing, all one and continuous,
> like any other organism, and in proportion as it lives will it be found, I think,
> that in each of the parts there is something of each of the other parts. The
> critic who over the close texture of a finished work shall pretend to trace a
> geography of items will mark some frontiers as artificial, I fear, as any that
> have been known to history.

Thus James indicts the critic who indulges in the use of such
notions as "description," "narration," "dialogue," etc., for committing two mistakes at the same time. 1. Supposing that such
abstract units can exist in the pure state in a work. 2. Daring to
use abstract notions, which pervert that intangible object (that
"living thing") that is the work of art.

The perspective taken by poetics deprives the first approach of
all its force: specifically, poetics situates these abstract notions not
within the particular work but in literary discourse; it asserts that
they can exist there alone, whereas in the work we always deal
with a more or less "mixed" manifestation; poetics is not concerned
with this or that fragment of a work, but with those abstract
structures which it names "description" or "action" or "narration."

The second argument is the more important and, moreover, by

far the more frequent. Even today, a *noli me tangere* still hangs over the work of art. There is something fascinating about this rejection of abstract thought. However, James need only have extended his already ambiguous comparison of the novel with a living organism in order to measure the limits of its effectiveness: in every "part" of our body, there are at once blood, muscles, lymph, and nerves: this does not keep us from employing all these terms and using them without anyone's protesting that we do so. We also hear it said: there are no diseases, only patients; fortunately for us, medicine has not followed this precept. But whom do we risk killing by defending absurd positions in literary studies? What is more: no one, not even Henry James, can avoid the use of descriptive terms, hence of a theory which warrants them; quite simply, we can retain this theory implicitly or argue it explicitly.

The fact that this essay was originally intended for a series of structuralist studies raises a new question: what is structuralism's relation to poetics? The difficulty of answering is proportional to the polysemy of the term "structuralism."

Taking this word in its broad acceptation, all poetics, and not merely one or another of its versions, is structural: since the object of poetics is not the sum of empirical phenomena (literary works) but an abstract structure (literature). But then, the introduction of a scientific point of view into any realm is always and already *structural.*

If on the other hand this word designates a limited corpus of hypotheses, one that is historically determined—thereby reducing language to a system of communication, or social phenomena to the products of a code—poetics, as presented here, has nothing particularly structuralist about it. We might even say that the literary phenomenon and, consequently, the discourse that assumes it (poetics), by their very existence, constitute an objection to certain instrumentalist conceptions of language formulated at the beginnings of "structuralism."

Which leads us to specify the relations between poetics and linguistics. For many "poeticians" in France, linguistics has played the part of a mediator with regard to the general methodology of scientific activity; it has been a (more or less well-attended) school of intellectual rigor, of discursive method, of procedural protocol. Nothing is more natural for two disciplines that result from the transformation of the same ancestor: philology. But we can also agree that this is a purely existential and contingent relation: in other circumstances, any other scientific discipline might have taken the same methodological role. There is another place, however, where this relation becomes, on the contrary, a necessary one: literature is, in the strongest sense of the term, a product of language. (Malarmé had said: "The book, total expansion of the letter. . . .") For this reason, any knowledge of language will be of interest to the poetician. But formulated this way, the relation unites poetics and linguistics less than it does literature and language: hence poetics and *all* the sciences of languages. Now, no more than poetics is the only science to take literature as its object is linguistics (at least as it exists today) the unique science of language. Its object is a certain type of linguistic structure (phonological, grammatical, semantic) to the exclusion of others, which are studied in anthropology, in psychoanalysis, or in "philosophy of language." Hence poetics might find a certain assistance in each of these sciences, to the degree that language constitutes part of their object. Its closest relatives will be the other disciplines that deal with *discourse* — the group forming the field of *rhetoric,* understood in the broadest sense as a general science of discourses.

It is here that poetics participates in the general semiotic project that unites all investigations whose point of departure is the *sign.*

Poetics will necessarily define its trajectory between two extremes, the very particular and the excessively general. It is burdened by an age-old tradition that, in the course of extremely varied arguments, always arrives at the same result: abandonment of all abstract reflection, confinement to the description of the specific and the singular. We have seen the necessary complementarity of the two procedures, which forbids any hierarchization;

yet if we emphasize poetics today, it is for purely strategic reasons: for each Lessing who describes the laws of fable, how many exegetes who explain the meaning of one fable or another! A massive imbalance in favor of interpretation characterizes the history of literary studies: it is this disequilibrium that we must oppose, and not the principle of interpretation.

A symmetrical and converse danger has appeared in recent years, a danger of over-theorization: in a movement that is itself in accord with the principles of poetics but skips all intermediary stages, increasingly formalized versions of poetics are being proposed, in a discourse that no longer has anything but itself for its object. This is to forget how slight is our most immediate knowledge of literary phenomena, how incomplete and clumsy our observations, how partial the facts we wield. This state of affairs obliges us to opt here for theory rather than for methodology; our object will be the discourse of literature, in preference to that of poetics; and before formalizing, we shall seek to conceptualize. We shall adopt that recent reflection of an American sociologist facing a comparable situation: "I assume that a loose speculative approach to a fundamental area of conduct is better than a rigorous blindness to it."

For the moment, poetics is only in its early stages; and it presents all the characteristic defects of such a stage. The contour of literary phenomena to be discerned here is still clumsy and inadequate: we are furnished with initial approximations, excessive and yet necessary simplifications. The account that follows offers, moreover, only a part of the investigations that can be legitimately inscribed within the context of poetics. Let us hope that the awkwardness of these first steps in a new direction will not be taken for the proof that this direction is the wrong one.

Chapter Two
Analysis of the Literary Text

i. Introduction: The Semantic Aspect

We read a book. We want to talk about it. What kind of phenomena can we observe, what type of questions will be raised?

The variety of phenomena and of problems appears such, at first glance, that we doubt the existence of any order whatever. But let us not feign innocence: discourse about literature is congenital to literature itself, and the question is not so much one of inventing an order as of choosing among the many possibilities available to us; of choosing in the least arbitrary manner possible.

First we shall divide the countless interrelationships to be observed in the literary text into two major groups: relations between copresent elements, *in praesentia;* relations between elements present and absent, *in absentia.* These relations differ as much in nature as in function.

As in any very general division, this one cannot be regarded as absolute. There are elements absent from the text that are to such a degree present in the collective memory of readers of a certain period that we are virtually dealing with a relation *in praesentia.* Conversely, segments of a sufficiently long book can be found at such a distance from each other that their relation is no different from a relation *in absentia.* Nonetheless, this opposition will

13

afford us a first regrouping of the constitutive elements of the literary work.

To what does it correspond in our experience as readers? The relations *in absentia* are relations of meaning and of symbolization. A certain signifier *signifies* a certain signified, a certain phenomenon *evokes* another, a certain episode *symbolizes* an idea, another *illustrates* a psychology. The relations *in praesentia* are relations of configuration, of construction. Here, it is by the power of a *causality* (not of an evocation) that the phenomena are linked to each other, the characters form among themselves *antitheses* and *gradations* (not symbolizations), the words *combine* into a new relation—in short, word, action, character neither signify nor symbolize those other words, actions, characters to which it is essential that they be *juxtaposed*. Linguistics deals with syntagmatic relations (*in praesentia*) and paradigmatic relations (*in absentia*), or with *syntax* and *semantics*.

Yet literature is not a "primary" symbolic system (as painting, for example, can be, or as a language is, in a sense) but "secondary": it utilizes as raw material an already existing system, language. This difference between linguistic system and literary system cannot be uniformly observed in every instance of literature: it is at its minimum in writings of "lyric" or sapiential type, in which the sentences of the text are organized directly among themselves; at its maximum in the text of fiction, in which the actions and characters evoked form in their turn a configuration relatively independent of the concrete sentences which cause us to know it. Yet however slight it may be, the difference always exists; whence the existence of a third series of problems, linked to the verbal representation of the fictional system (which we can, ultimately, imagine represented by another medium, such as film); which compels us to take into consideration the *verbal* aspect of the literary text.

Thus we may group into three sections the problems of literary analysis, according to whether they concern the verbal, the syntactic, or the semantic aspect of the text. This subdivision, though bearing different names and formulated, in detail, according to different points of view, has long been present in our realm. For example, the old rhetoric used to divide its field into *elocutio* (verbal), *dispositio* (syntactic), and *inventio* (semantic); again, the Russian Formalists distributed the field of literary studies into stylistics, composition, and thematics; finally, in contemporary linguistic theory we distinguish phonology, syntax, and semantics. These coincidences nonetheless conceal differences that are occasionally profound, and we can judge as to the content of the terms proposed here only after their description.

The three aspects of the literary text are very unequally familiar; we might almost characterize the different periods of the history of poetics according to whether the specialists' attention favors one or another aspect of the work.

The syntactic aspect (what Aristotle called, in the case of tragedy, the "quantitative parts") has been most neglected, until the close scrutiny to which the Russian Formalists subjected it in the 1920s; subsequently it has been at the center of attention, particularly in the case of those investigators identified with the "structural" tendency.

The verbal aspect of literature has benefited from the attention of several recent critical tendencies: "style" has been studied in the context of stylistics; "modes" of narration in the context of morphological investigations in Germany; "viewpoints," in the tradition of Henry James, in England and in the United States.

The case is somewhat different with regard to what we are calling the semantic aspect of the text. In a sense, all *interpretations* put this aspect in the foreground, hence it is the most abundantly treated. But almost never in the perspective of poetics: the meaning of a certain work is discussed, not the general conditions of the genesis of meaning. We cannot, in the context of this account, alter the situation: we should have to invent, where our ambition is merely to present and to systematize. But in order to avoid too great an imbalance, granted that our later chapters will be devoted to the description of the syntactic and verbal aspects, we shall try, in the following pages, to present in brief the semantic problematics of the literary text.

If the theory of literary semantics remains at an impasse for the moment, one reason is that very different phenomena, though all dealing with "semantics," have been jumbled together. Our task then will be, first of all, to distinguish the problems (rather than to solve them).

Initially we must isolate two types of semantic questions: formal and substantial; i.e., *how does a text signify?* and *what does a text signify?*

The first question occupies the center of attention of linguistic semantics. It happens however that the linguistic approach suffers from two limitations: it confines itself, on the one hand, solely to "meaning," in the strict sense, leaving aside all problems of connotation, of the lucid use of language, of metaphorization; on the other hand, it rarely exceeds the limits of the sentence, the basic linguistic unit. Now, these two aspects of formal semantics, "second" meanings and the signifying organization of "discourse," are especially pertinent to literary analysis; and they have long since attracted the attention of specialists. What do we know about them today?

The study of meanings other than the "literal" meaning traditionally constituted part of rhetoric, more specifically to be found under the heading *tropes.* Nowadays we no longer sustain the opposition between proper and derived meaning, whether of historical or normative origin; but we distinguish the process of *signification* (in which a signifier means a signified) from that of *symbolization,* in which a first signified symbolizes a second; signification is given in vocabulary (in the paradigms of words), symbolization occurs in discourse (the syntagm). The interaction between the first meaning and the second (sometimes called, following I. A. Richards, "vehicle" and "tenor") is not a simple substitution, nor a predication, but a specific relation, whose modalities are only beginning to be studied, as by Empson. What is— relatively speaking—better known is the abstract variety of the relations occurring between the two meanings: classical rhetoric gave them the names *synechdoche, metaphor, metonymy, antiphrasis, hyperbole, litotes;* modern rhetoric has sought to interpret these relations in logical terms such as inclusion, exclusion, intersection, etc.

As for the symbolic properties of segments superior to the sentence, we must know whether or not the symbolism is an intratextual one. If it is, one part of the text designates another: a character will indeed be "characterized" by his actions or by descriptive details, an abstract reflection will be "illustrated" by the totality of the plot (in a sense, the first sentence of *Anna Karenina* contains the rest of the book in condensed form). In the second case—if the symbolism is not intratextual—we are dealing with exegesis in the current sense, i.e., with the passage between the literary text and the critical text (this is what the total act of interpretation is habitually reduced to): exegesis will itself be circumscribed by various *hermeneutics* or abstract rules that govern its functioning. The most highly elaborated of these, in Western tradition, is that which has been formed around the reading of the Bible. Hermeneutics is not always concerned with the description of its procedures; it is possible that on this transphrastic level we may still discover the same tropical categories, the same problems of interaction of meanings (allegory was a figure before being a genre); but as yet we possess only partial knowledge with regard to everything that concerns the symbolic structure of discourses.

The second major question, the one that defines substantial semantics, is: what is signified? Here again, it is important to distinguish problems often treated together.

We may first ask to what degree the literary text *describes* the world (its referent); in other words, we may raise the problem of its truth. To say that the literary text refers to a reality, that this reality constitutes its referent, is in effect to establish a relation of *truth* and to assume the submission of literary discourse to the test of truth, the right to say that it is true or false. Now, a rather odd convergence *and* opposition can be observed on this point between the logicians, specialists in problems raised by the relation of truth, and the first theoreticians of the novel. The latter were in the habit of setting *history* in opposition to the novel, or to other literary genres, in order to say that if the former should be always true, the latter could even be entirely false. Thus Pierre-Daniel Huet wrote in his *Traité de l'origine des romans* that novels "can even be entirely untrue, both in design and in detail." From here it was only a step to discern the resemblance of novels and lies, feigned speech; the same Huet sees the origin of the novel among the Arabs, apparently a race especially gifted for lying.

Modern logic (since Frege, at least) has more or less rejected this judgment: literature is not a discourse that can or must be false, in contrast to the discourse of the sciences; it is a discourse that, precisely, cannot be subjected to the test of truth; it is neither true nor false, to raise this question has no meaning: this is what defines its very status as "fiction."

Logically speaking, then, no sentence of the literary text is either true or false. Which of course does not keep the work as a whole from possessing a certain descriptive power: to extremely diverse degrees, novels evoke "life," as it has actually unfolded. It is therefore possible, when we study a society, to make use of literary texts, among other documents. But the absence of a rigorous relation of truth must at the same time make us extremely cautious: the text can "reflect" social life but can just as well incarnate its exact opposite. Such a perspective is quite legitimate, but leads us beyond poetics: by putting literature on the same level as any other document, we are obviously no longer concerned with its specifically literary qualities.

This problem of relation between literature and extra-literary phenomena has often been confused, under the name "realism," with another, which is the individual text's conformity to a textual norm external to it; this conformity produces the *illusion* of realism and makes us say such a text possesses *verisimilitude.*

If we study the discussions bequeathed us by the past, we realize that a work is said to have verisimilitude in relation to two chief kinds of norms. The first is what we call the *rules of the genre:* for a work to be said to have verisimilitude, it must conform to these rules. In certain periods, a comedy is judged "probable" only if, in the last act, the characters are discovered to be near relations. A sentimental novel will be probable if its outcome consists in the marriage of hero and heroine, if virtue is rewarded and vice punished. Verisimilitude, taken in this sense, designates the work's relation to literary discourse: more exactly, to certain of the latter's subdivisions, which form a genre.

But there exists another verisimilitude, which has been taken even more frequently for a relation with reality. Aristotle, however, had already perceived that the verisimilar is not a relation between discourse and its referent (the relation of truth), but between discourse and what readers believe is true. The relation is here established between the work and a scattered discourse that in part belongs to each of the individuals of a society but of which none may claim ownership; in other words, to *public opinion*. The latter is of course not "reality" but merely a further discourse, independent of the work. Public opinion therefore functions as a rule of genre that relates to all genres.

The opposition between these two types of verisimilitude is irreducible only at first glance. Once we adopt the historical viewpoint, what we find is something quite different: the successive diversity of the rules of genre. Public opinion is only one genre, which claims to prevail over all the others; the actual genres admit, on the contrary, diversity and coexistence.

It is useful to confront, in this perspective, the doctrine of classicism with that of nineteenth-century naturalism. On the one hand, classical poetics refers explicitly to the rules of genre without claiming that conformity to them equals truth. The poet "must rather change [truth] altogether," Chapelain writes, "than leave anything about it incompatible with the rules of his art." On the other hand, the theoreticians of classicism willingly admit the existence of several genres and, consequently, of several versimilitudes. The various means at the poet's disposal can all contribute to verisimilitude, but in different genres. Horace had already written in his *Ars poetica* that iambic verse suits satire, the "distich of lines of unequal length" suits lament and gratitude, etc. As for public opinion, it has different rights in the different genres: the poem "though always verisimilar," Huet will say, "is less so than the novel." In other words, the law of certain genres coincides with public opinion; but the latter does not have absolute rights.

The doctrine of naturalism is situated at the opposite pole. The naturalists do not admit that they are referring to rules of genre; their writings must be *true*, not just likely. Actually, this signifies that the only rule admitted is that of public opinion. The direct consequence of this principle is the reduction of all genres to only one; if the rules of a genre contradict this verisimilitude, the genre is suppressed: in the doctrine of naturalism, there is no place for the poem. Thus, speaking of poetry, the Russian realist Saltykov-Shchedrin says: "I don't understand why one must walk a tight-rope and squat every three steps as well." From this comparison we can conclude that naturalism rejects, in theory at least, the variety of discourses; yet the recognition of this variety and the successive elaboration of a veritable typology is a necessary condition for knowledge of the text.

Finally, it is to a third field that what we might call the hypothesis of a general literary thematics belongs. For a very long time, investigations have been made into the possibility of presenting the themes of literature not as an open and disorderly series but as a structured set. For the time being, most of these attempts have taken as their point of departure an organization external to literature: the cycles of nature, or the structure of the human psyche, etc.; we may wonder if it is not preferable to establish this hypothesis within language and within literature. The fact remains that the very existence of such a general thematics is far from being proved.

ii. Registers of Discourse

"The literary work consists of words," a critic would say today, seeking to acknowledge the importance of language in literature. But the literary work consists of words no more than any other linguistic utterance: it consists of sentences, and these sentences belong to different *registers* of discourse (a notion approached by certain uses of the word "style"). Their description will be our first task, for we must begin by seeing what linguistic means are at the writer's disposal, we must know what the properties of discourse are before their integration into a work. This preliminary study of the linguistic properties of preliterary materials is necessary to the knowledge of literary discourse itself, which we shall deal with subsequently: especially since there exists no impassable frontier between the former and the latter.

We shall make no attempt to summarize here the already

numerous investigations of "styles"; rather, we shall attempt to emphasize only several categories, whose presence or absence creates a register of language. Moreover we must also add immediately that it is never a matter of an absolute presence or absence, but of quantitative predominances (which, furthermore, it is extremely difficult to measure: how many metaphors must there be to a page before we can qualify a style as "metaphorical"?): these are not true oppositions but graduated and continuous characteristics.

1. A first very obvious category that allows us to characterize a register is what we call, in everyday usage, its "concrete" or "abstract" nature. At one of the extremes of this continuum are found the sentences whose subject designates a singular, material, and discontinuous being; at the other, the "general" reflections that enunciate a "truth"outside of any spatial or temporal reference. Between these two extremes is located an infinity of transition-cases, depending on whether the object evoked is more or less abstract. Intuitively, the reader always reacts to this property of the discourse, endowing it with different degrees of value: the realistic novel, for example, specializes in the presentation of material details (everyone remembers, Léons fingernails in *Madame Bovary*, or Anna Karenina's arm); the romantic novel, on the other hand, favors "analysis," lyric flights, abstract reflections (though every sort of mixture of the two is possible).

2. A second category, quite as familiar but more problematic, is determined by the presence of rhetorical figures (relations *in praesentia* to be distinguished from tropes, relations *in absentia*): this is the degree of a discourse's *figurality*. But what is a figure? If many theories have sought a common denominator for all figures, they have almost always been obliged to exclude certain figures from their field in order to be able to explain the others by the definition proposed. As a matter of fact, this definition should not be sought in the relation of the figure with something other than itself, but in its existence itself: a figure is what permits itself to be described as such. The figure is nothing but a particular disposition of words, which we can name and describe. If the relations of two words are of identity, there is a figure: *repetition*. If they

are of opposition, there is again a figure: *antithesis.* If one word denotes a quantity greater or lesser than the other, we shall still speak of a figure: *gradation.* But if the relation of the two words cannot be named by any of these terms, if it is still different, we shall then declare that this discourse is not figured or figurative; until the day when a new rhetorician teaches us how to describe this imperceptible relation.

Every relation of two (or several) copresent words can therefore become a figure; but this possibility is realized only when the receiver of the discourse perceives the figure (since it is nothing but *the discourse perceived as such*). This perception will be guaranteed either by recourse to schemas readily available to our mind (whence the frequency of figures based on repetition, symmetry, opposition), or by a particular insistence in the presentation of certain verbal relations: hence Jakobson could identify a great number of previously unknown "grammatical figures," relying upon an exhaustive analysis of the linguistic fabric of some particular poem.

The contrary of the figure, transparency—the invisibility of language—exists only as a limit (to which we come closest, probably, in the case of a purely utilitarian, functional discourse); a limit which it is necessary to conceive but which we must not attempt to grasp in the pure state. Try as we will to consider words as the simple garment of an ideal body, Peirce tells us that this garment can never be completely shed, but only exchanged for another that is more diaphanous. Language cannot vanish completely, becoming a pure mediator of meaning.

The theory of figures constituted one of the essential chapters of the old rhetoric. Under the stimulus of contemporary linguistics, several attempts have been made to provide a more coherent basis for the rich but chaotic catalog that our past has bequeathed to us. One of the most popular theories of the figure (which goes back, moreover, at least to Quintilian) envisages it as the infraction of one or another of the linguistic rules (theory of deviation).

Such a definition permits a more precise description of certain figures; but it comes up against serious objections as soon as we seek to extend it to the whole of the domain.

3. Another category that permits us to identify different "registers" within language is the presence or absence of reference to an anterior discourse. We might call this discourse *monovalent* (and it, too, can be conceived only as a limit) when it invokes no anterior "way of speaking"; and *polyvalent* when it invokes an anterior discourse more or less explicitly.

Classical literary history has treated this second type of writing with suspicion. The only authorized form was that which mocks and disparages the properties of the anterior discourse: parody. If the critical nuance is absent from this second discourse, the historian of literature speaks of "plagiarism." The relation between the two is not, of course, one of simple equivalence, but reveals great variety; and the interplay with the other text should in no case be obliterated. The words of a polyvalent discourse send us in two directions; to deprive it of one or the other is to fail to understand it altogether.

Let us take a familiar example: the story of the wounded knee in *Tristam Shandy* (VIII,20), repeated in *Jacques le Fataliste*. There is of course no question of plagiarism here, but rather of a dialogue. A number of details are changed, so that Diderot's text, though very close to Sterne's, is not comprehensible if we do not take into account the discrepancy between the two. Thus Jacques is offered "a bottle of wine" and he drinks off "one or two draughts, straightway"; this gesture assumes its full meaning if we recall that Trim had been offered "several drops [of cordial] on a lump of sugar." This correspondence was quite obvious for the contemporary reader (and Diderot himself indicates it); we cannot understand the text without taking into account its double signification: it signifies the woman's very gesture as well as Sterne's text.

It is thanks to the Russian Formalists that we have begun to recognize the importance of this feature of language. Shklovski had written: "The work of art is perceived in relation with other artisitic works and by means of the associations the reader makes with them. . . . Not only parody and pastiche, but every work of art is created in parallel with and in opposition to some model." But it was Bakhtin who first formulated a true theory of intertextual polyvalence; he asserts:

The element of the so-called reaction to the foregoing literary style which is present in every new style is also in its way an inner polemic or, so to speak, a hidden anti-stylization of the other style, and often combines with an obvious parody of that style. . . . For the prose artist the world is full of the words of other people, among which he orients himself and for the specific characteristics of which he must have a keen ear. . . . When each member of a collective of speakers takes possession of a word, it is not a neutral word of language, free from the aspirations and valuations of others, uninhabited by foreign voices. No, he receives the word from the voice of another, and the word arrives in his context from another context which is saturated with other people's interpretations. His own thought finds the word already inhabited (pp. 163-67).

In a similar perspective, more recently, Harold Bloom, instituting a psychoanalysis of literary history, has spoken of an "anxiety of influence" suffered by every writer when it is his turn to wield his language (his pen): he always writes for or against another's already existing book (and the trajectory from "for" to "against" sustains an infinite variety of nuances); others' voices inhabit his discourse, which thereby becomes "polyvalent."

When the present text evokes not another individual text but an an anonymous ensemble of discursive properties, we are faced with a different version of polyvalence. In his pioneering work, Milman Parry formulated this hypothesis concerning traditional oral poetry (Homeric verse as well as that of the Yugoslav bards): the epithet is attached to a substantive not in order to specify its meaning but because the two are traditionally associated; the metaphor is not there to increase the semantic density of the text, but because it belongs to the arsenal of poetic ornaments and because, in using it, the text signifies its adherence to literature or to one of its subdivisions. But Parry regarded this feature as characteristic only of oral literature, imposed by the bards' obligation to improvise, hence to draw on a reservoir of ready-made formulas. It has since been possible to extend this hypothesis to written literature; this extension has involved a restriction as to the nature of what is "evoked." The new text is not produced with the help of a series of elements belonging roughly to "literature," but by reference to more specific ensembles: a certain style, a particular tradition, a type of usage or of poetic procedure. It is to Michael Riffaterre that we owe this transformation of Parry's hypothesis concerning formulaic poetic language. This leads us to a generalized theory of the cliché, which can just as well be stylistic as thematic or narrative, and which plays a determinative part in the constitution of the meaning of a discourse. Phenomena of this same type, but within the spoken language, had been described by the founder of modern stylistics, Charles Bally, as *effects of evocation by milieu*. For example, the word *gat*, in opposition to *revolver*, evokes a milieu for us, or the texts that describe it. Again we have given here only a few among the numerous varieties of polyvalent discourse.

4. The last feature we shall list here to characterize the variety of verbal registers is what we might call, following Benveniste, the "subjectivity" of language (as opposed to its "objectivity"). Every discourse bears traces of the personal and individual act of its production; but such traces can be more or less intense. To give but one example, the French *passé simple* confers a minimum of subjectivity upon discourse: all we can know is that the action described is anterior to the act of description (such as the faint trace left here by "subjectivity").

The linguistic forms such "traces" take are numerous, and they have been the object of a number of descriptions. We might distinguish two chief series: indications as to the speaker's identity and as to the spatio-temporal coordinates of the speech-act habitually transmitted by specialized *morphemes* (pronouns or verb endings); and indications as to the attitude of the speaker and/or of the hearer with regard to the discourse or its object (which constitutes only *semes,* aspects of the meaning of other words). It is by just this means that the total speech-act penetrates all verbal statements: each sentence involves an indication as to its speaker's dispositions. Someone who says "This book is beautiful" makes a value judgment and thereby introduces himself between the utterance and its referent; but someone who says "This tree is tall" offers a judgment of the same kind, though less obvious, and informs us, for example, about the flora of his own country. Every sentence involves an evaluation, though to different degrees, which allows us to oppose an "evaluative" discourse to the other registers of discourse.

Within this subjective register have been distinguished several classes with more rigorously defined properties. The best known is *emotive* (or *expressive) discourse,* the classic study of which is by Charles Bally. Many subsequent investigations have isolated its manifestations in phonic, graphic, grammatical, and lexical features.

Another type of subjectivity is achieved in a clearly isolated sector of vocabulary: this is *modalizing discourse,* to which the modal verbs and adverbs (*can, should; perhaps, certainly,* etc.) refer. Once again the subject of the speech-act, and through it the entire action, are made evident.

The interpenetration of all these registers in the concrete text cannot be exaggerated. Contemporary literature furnishes us with new and particularly complex cases. Here for example is a passage from *Ulysses:*

"His smile faded as he walked, a heavy cloud hiding the sun slowly, shadowing Trinity's surly front. Trams passed one another, ingoing, outgoing, clanging. Useless words. Things go on the same, day after day: squads of police marching out, back: trams in, out. Those two loonies mooching about. Dignam carted off."

The first sentence of this text seems to belong to an objective narrative; but is it Bloom who thinks "surly" or the narrator who says it? Without visible break, the sentences following "Useless words" emphasize the speech-act itself: it is Bloom who thinks, and his thought is presented in an "interior monologue," a form that combines several characteristics of emotive or evaluative registers: hence nominal sentences, ellipses, present tense, inversions, etc.

This list of the registers of discourse cannot claim to be exhaustive: its goal is merely to give an image of their variety as utilized in the work of fiction. Nor does it offer a coherent and logical system: to achieve such a result, we should require many more investigations based on the knowledge granted by linguistics. But a reading cannot be rigorous if it ignores these resources of discourse available to literature. Contemporary literature, in particular, unceasingly obliges us to take them into account: it is not content to make their very distribution within the work coincide with that of another structure formed by the plot, in order to reinforce the latter; rather it is this distribution that affords the work's total and primary organization, the other levels of the text obeying this one.

iii. The Verbal Aspect: Mode, Time

After reviewing those linguistic properties of a discourse whose systematic presence creates a "register," we must now turn to what constitutes the essential of the "verbal aspect" of literature: a problematics related to and yet distinct from the foregoing.

The work of fiction effects the transition—whose omnipresence conceals its importance and its singularity—from a series of sentences to an imaginary universe. Once we turn the last page of *Madame Bovary*, we remain in contact with a certain number of characters, whose destiny we more or less know; yet what we had between our hands was only a linear discourse. We must not yield to the representative illusion that has so long helped to conceal this metamorphosis: there is not, *first of all*, a certain reality, *and afterward*, its representation by the text. The given is the literary text; starting from it, by a labor of *construction*—which occurs in the reader's mind but is in no way individual, since such constructions are analogous in various readers—we reach that universe where certain characters live, comparable to the persons we know "in life."

This metamorphosis of discourse into fiction can occur as the consequence of a certain amount of information contained by the discourse: an amount necessarily incomplete (this is the "schematism" of the literary text, mentioned by Ingarden), for "things" are never exhausted by their name; and because of this absence of any absolute, there are a thousand "ways" of evoking the same thing. Such information will be modulated and qualified according to several parameters. The distinction of such parameters will allow us to articulate the problem of the "verbal aspect" of literary fiction.

In the present account, we shall distinguish three types of properties that characterize information allowing us to shift from discourse to fiction. The category of *mode* concerns the degree of presence of the events evoked in the text. The category of *time* concerns the relation between two temporal lines: that of the fictional discourse (figured for us by the linear linking of the letters on the page and the pages in the volume) and that of the (much more complex) fictive universe. Finally the category of perspective or *vision* (I also use this latter term, which is in common use today, despite certain undesirable connotations): the point of view from which we observe the object and the quality of this observation (true or false, partial or complete). To these three categories we shall add a fourth no longer located on the same level but, in the phenomena themselves, inextricably linked to them: this is the presence of the speech-act as a whole in the discourse, which we have just examined, in the preceding chapter, on the stylistic level; it will here be considered from the point of view of the fiction, and we shall refer to it by the term *voice*.

The category of *mode* brings us back to the verbal registers we were examining above; but the point of view is different here. The text of fiction must necessarily be situated in relation to the following problem: we evoke by words a universe that consists in part of words and in part of nonverbal activities (or substances, or properties); consequently the relation will not be the same between the discourse (which we read) and either another discourse or a nondiscursive substance.

This distinction was designated in classical poetics (in Plato, to begin with) by the terms *mimesis* (narrative of words) and *diegesis* (of "non-words"). Strictly speaking, we are not justified in evoking any mimesis whatever (except in the marginal case of imitative harmony): words, we know, are "unmotivated." In the first instance, it is rather a matter of *insertion* into the present text of words supposedly pronounced or formulated for themselves; in the second, of the *designation* of nonverbal phenomena by words (which is always and necessarily "arbitrary").

Therefore the narrative of nonverbal events knows no modal varieties (but only historical variants, which produce with more or less success, depending on the conventions of the period, the illusion of "realism"): in no way do things bear their name inscribed within themselves. On the other hand, the narrative of words includes several species, for words can be "inserted" with more or less exactitude.

Gérard Genette has suggested that we distinguish three degrees of insertion: 1. The *direct* style: here the discourse undergoes no modification; we speak sometimes of "reported discourse." 2. The *indirect* style (or "*transposed* discourse") in which we retain the "content" of the discourse supposedly uttered but integrate it grammatically into the speaker's narrative. Moreover the changes are often more than grammatical: we abridge, we eliminate affective judgments, etc. A variant between direct and indirect style is what in French is called "free indirect style": here the grammatical forms of the indirect style are adopted, but the semantic nuances of the "original" discourse are retained, especially all indications concerning the subject of the speech-act; there is no declarative verb introducing and qualifying the transposed sentence. 3. The final degree of transformation of the character's words is what we might call "*recounted* discourse": here we are content to register the content of the speech-act without retaining any of its elements. Let us imagine this sentence: "I informed my mother of my decision to marry Albertine"; it indicates clearly that there has been a verbal action, as well as the tenor of that action; but we know nothing of the words that were "really" (i.e., fictively) uttered.

The mode of a discourse therefore consists in the degree of exactitude with which this discourse evokes its referent: a maximum degree in the case of direct style, a minimum degree in the case of the narrative of nonverbal phenomena; intermediary degrees in the other cases.

Another aspect of the information that enables us to shift from discourse to fiction is *time.* There exists a "problem of time" because two temporalities are found juxtaposed: that of the universe represented and that of the discourse representing it. This difference between the order of events and the order of words is an obvious one, but literary theory took it fully into account only when the Russian Formalists employed it as one of the chief indices in order to set the *fable* (order of events) in opposition to the *subject* (order of discourse); more recently, a tendency of literary studies in Germany has made this opposition between *Erzälzeit* and *erzählte Zeit* the basis of its doctrine.

These phenomenon of temporality have lately constituted the object of careful studies, which will free us from having to insist upon them at length here; we shall merely indicate the main problems that arise in this context.

1. The easiest relation to observe is that of *order:* the order of narrating time (the order of discourse) can never be perfectly parallel to the order of time narrated (of fiction); there are necessarily interversions in the "before" and the "after." These interversions are due to the difference in nature between the two temporalities: that of discourse is one-dimensional, that of fiction, plural. The impossibility of parallelism therefore leads to *anachronias,* of which we may note two evident aspects: *retrospections,* or backward looks, and *prospections,* or anticipations. There is prospection when we announce in advance what will happen later: the canonical example given by the Formalists was Tolstoy's tale *The Death of Ivan Ilyich,* which contains its outcome in its title. Retrospections, more frequent in fiction, tell us *afterward* what has happened *earlier:* in classical narrative, the introduction of a new character is habitually followed by an account of his past, if not by an evocation of his ancestors. In theory these two aspects can be combined to infinity (retrospection in prospection in retrospection . . .: cf. this sentence of Proust cited by Genette: "Many years later we learned that if that summer we had eaten asparagus almost every day, it was because their odor gave the poor kitchen-girl whose job it was to peel them such violent asthma attacks that she was forced, finally, to leave her job"). Further, we can distinguish between the *context* of the anachronia (the temporal distance between two moments of fiction) and its *amplitude* (duration enveloped by the narrative given as a digression); depending on whether or not the anachronia intersects with the main narrative, we can qualify it as *internal* or *external.* The (necessarily) successive narrative of two simultaneous events will be, for instance, an "internal" anachronia of no extent whatever.

2. From the perspective of *duration*, we can compare the time that the action represented is supposed to last with the time we require to read the discourse that evokes it. As a matter of fact, this latter time cannot be measured as by a stopwatch, and we must always speak in relative values. Several cases can be clearly distinguished, however: 1. The suspension of time, or *pause*, occurs when no fictional time corresponds to the time of discourse: this will be the case with description, general reflections, etc. 2. The opposite case is the one in which no portion of discursive time corresponds to the time that passes in the fiction: this is obviously the omission of a whole period, or *ellipsis*. 3. We already know the third fundamental case, that of a perfect coincidence between the two time sequences: it can be achieved only through the direct style, insertion of the fictive reality into the discourse, thereby producing a *scene*. 4. Finally, two intermediary cases are conceivable: those in which the time of discourse is "longer" or "shorter" than that of fiction. It seems that the former variant infallibly returns us to two other possibilities already encountered, descriptions or anachronia (for instance, the twenty-four hours in the life of Leopold Bloom which we would have difficulty *reading* in twenty-four hours: what "swells" the time are precisely the achronias and the anachronias). The latter is frequently encountered: it is the résumé or *summary*, which condenses whole years into a sentence.

3. A final essential property of the relation between discourse-time and fiction-time is *frequency*. Three theoretical possibilities are offered here: a *singulative* narrative in which a unique discourse evokes a unique event; a *repetitive* narrative, in which several discourses evoke one and the same event; finally an *iterative* discourse, in which a single discourse evokes a plurality of (similar) events. The singulative narrative needs no commentary. The repetitive narrative can result from various processes: obsessive reprise of the same story by the same character; complementary narratives by several persons about the same phenomenon (which creates a "stereoscopic" illusion); contradictory narratives by one or several characters, which make us doubt the reality or the exact tenor of a particular event. We know the use made of this method by eighteenth-century British novelists, especially in

their epistolary works (Richardson, Smollett); in *Les Liaisons dangereuses,* Laclos uses the device to disclose the naïveté of some of his characters (Cécile, Danceny, Mme de Tourvel), the perfidy of others (Valmont, Madame de Merteuil). Such methods obviously involve other elements of the "verbal aspect"; we may note here the necessary temporal "distortion" that results, since a succession of events no longer corresponds to the succession of discourses.

The iterative narrative, finally, which consists in designating by a single discourse (a sentence) events that are repeated, is a procedure known to all classical literature, where it nonetheless plays a limited part: the writer habitually evokes an initial stable condition with the help of verbs in the imperfect tense (of an iterative value), before introducing the series of singular events that will constitute his narrative proper. As Genette has shown, Proust is one of the first to have granted the iterative a dominant role—to such a degree that we find narrated in this mode phenomena that certainly could not occur more than once (Proust creates a "pseudo-iterative": hence there are certain conversations that probably could not be repeated without alteration, and that Proust nonetheless introduces by formulas of this type: "And if Swann used to ask her what she meant by that, she would answer him a little scornfully. . . ." etc.). The total effect of this method can be a certain suspension of contingent time.

iv. The Verbal Aspect: Perspective, Voice

The third major category that allows us to characterize the shift from discourse to fiction is that of perspective or *vision:* the phenomena that compose the fictive universe are never presented to us "in themselves" but from a certain perspective, a certain point of view, etc. This visual vocabulary is metaphorical, or rather synechdochic: "vision" here replaces total perception; but it is a convenient metaphor, for the many characteristics of "real" vision all have equivalents in the phenomenon of fiction.

Not much attention was paid to the problem of perspective before the beginning of the twentieth century, which doubtless explains, starting at this period, why it was supposed that the very secret of literary art was hidden here. Percy Lubbock's book, the first study systematically devoted to this question, is called, significantly, *The Craft of Fiction*. And indeed, the question of viewpoints is of the first importance. We never deal, in literature, with events or facts in the raw, but with events presented in a certain fashion. Two different visions of the same phenomenon constitute two distinct phenomena. All the aspects of an object are determined by the vision we are afforded of it. This importance has always been acknowledged in the visual arts, and literary theory has much to learn from the theory of painting. To cite but one example among others, specialists have often remarked the presence of perspectives and their decisive role for the picture's structure in Byzantine icons: it is evident that several points of view are utilized within one and the same icon, according to the part that the figure represented is to play: the chief figure is turned toward the spectator, whereas, according to the scene represented, this figure should be turned toward his or her interlocutor.

It is important to note that literary perspectives do not concern the reader's real perception, which always remains variable and depends on factors external to the work, but a perception presented within this work, although in a specific mode. Here again, the history of painting affords us eloquent examples. We need merely recall those *anamorphic* pictures, coded compositions, incomprehensible when seen straight on, the most frequent point of view; but which, from a particular point of view (usually parallel to the picture), offer the image of familiar objects. This distortion between a point of view inherent in the work and the most frequent point of view emphasizes the former's reality as well as the importance of visions for comprehension of the work.

There exist various descriptions of perspective in literature: we might even say that this is the aspect most attentively studied in this century by poetics. Following Lubbock's book, we should mention here, however summarily, such works as Jean Pouillon's *Temps et roman;* Wayne Booth's *Rhetoric of Fiction;* B. Uspenski's *Poètika kompzicii;* and Gérard Genette's "Discours du Récit." These investigations have shed light on many aspects of our problem, and must be consulted for any more detailed discussion. For our part, we shall be concerned here—contrary to most of the studies cited—not with the description of particular kinds of perspective, but with the description of the categories which permit the distinction among these kinds. Each example of perspective in effect, as it has been studied till now, combines several distinct characteristics which it will be to our advantage to examine in succession.

1. The first category is that of our *subjective* or *objective* knowledge of the events represented. A perception informs us about what is perceived as well as about the perceiver: it is the first type of information that we are calling objective, the second, subjective. We must not confuse this phenomenon with the possibility of presenting an entire narrative "in the first person": whether the narration is conducted in the first or the third person, it can always furnish us the two types of information. Henry James called the characters who are not only perceived but also perceiving, "reflectors": if the other characters are above all images reflected in a consciousness, the reflector is that consciousness itself. To give but one example of this: in Proust's novel, we derive most of our information about Marcel not from his actions but from the way in which he perceives and judges those of others.

2. This first category that concerns, on the whole, the *direction* of the work of construction in which the reader engages (starting from a perception, we turn toward its subject or toward its object) must be clearly distinguished from a second category, which no longer concerns the quality but the quantity of information received, or, we may say, the reader's degree of *knowledge*. Still abiding by the visual metaphor, we can separate, within this second category, two distinct notions: the *extent* (or the angle) of vision, and its *depth* or the degree of its penetration.

As for "extent," the two extreme poles are habitually designated as *internal* and *external* vision, or again "from inside" and "from outside." As it happens, purely "external" vision, the one that confines itself to describing actions perceptible without accompanying them with any interpretation, any incursion into the protagonist's mind, never exists in the pure state: it would lead into the unintelligible.

Moreover it is no accident that this technique has met with such an extended use in the detective fiction of Dashiell Hammett, where it serves to reinforce mystery. Hence it is a question less of an internal/external opposition than of degrees in the presence of the "internal." The most internal vision would be the one afforded by *all* a character's thoughts. Thus in *Les Liaisons dangereuses*, Valmont and Merteuil see the other characters "from inside," whereas the little Volanges girl can only describe or misinterpret the behavior of those around her. The contrast is as strong between the perspectives of Quentin and Benjy in *The Sound and the Fury*.

We shall distinguish the "angle" of vision thus defined from its "depth": we may not be content to accept the "surface," whether physical or psychological; we may instead want to penetrate the characters' unconscious intentions, to present a dissection of their minds (of which they themselves would not be capable).

Let us take an example illustrating these two categories of "direction" and "knowledge": "Meanwhile he stared at Madame Dambreuse, and charming he found her, though her mouth was a little too wide and her nostrils too open. But her grace was a special one. The curls on her head had a kind of languid passion about them, and her agate-colored brow seemed to contain so many things, betokening a master" *(A Sentimental Education)*.

Here we have a certain amount of objective information about Madame Dambreuse, and of subjective information about Frédéric, which we derive from his way of perceiving and interpreting. The perception of Madame Dambreuse occurs according to a relatively reduced angle of vision: we are given only certain physical qualities. Frédéric advances several interpretations; but we note how cautiously they are introduced: "languid passion" is preceded by "a kind of," her brow "seems" to contain and "betokens" (a verb equivalent to "signify," not to "be"). Thus Flaubert authenticates none of his "reflector's" suppositions.

3. Here we must introduce two categories that will permit us to establish certain subspecies of perspectives but that have nothing "optical" about them, strictly speaking: these are the oppositions between unicity and multiplicity, on the one hand; consistency and variability, on the other. In effect, each of the preceding categories can be modulated according to these new parameters: *only one* character can be seen "from inside" (and this

leads to "internal focusing"), or *all* the characters—which produces narrative with an "omniscient narrator." The second case is
that of Boccaccio: in the *Decameron,* the narrator knows the intentions of all the characters equally. The former is that of the
modern novel; the principle has been applied with particular rigor
by Henry James. Similarly, an internal vision can be applied to a
character throughout the narrative or during only one of its parts
(as is the case with John Cowper Powys's *Maiden Castle*); and
these changes in vision may or may not be systematic. If for
instance James sees several characters "from inside" in the course
of the same novel, the shift from one to the next follows a rigorous design that sometimes forms the very armature of the book.
But James's practice in no way signifies that this case is the most
widespread—or even the most desirable.

Let us also note with Uspenski that the change in point of view
—in particular the shift from an external vision to an internal
one—assumes a function comparable to that of the frame in the
painting: it serves as a transition between the work and its envi-
ronment (the "nonwork").

4. Our information concerning the fictive universe can be of an
objective or subjective nature; it can be more or less extended
(internal and external); but there is still one more dimension by
which we must characterize it: it can be *absent* or *present* and, in
this last case, *true* or *false*. We have hitherto spoken as if this
information was always true; but it would have sufficed for
Frédéric to misinterpret Madame Dambreuse's curls and for us
to have granted him a blind confidence, for us to find ourselves
confronting not information but an illusion. This imperfect vision
is not necessarily accompanied by the character's *mistake:* it may
be a matter of a deliberate *dissimulation.*

In order to believe in an illusion, we must possess a certain
amount of information, however abusive. The extreme case is
equally possible—of a total absence of information: we are no
longer in illusion, but in *ignorance.* Let us not forget, at the same
time, that no description is ever complete, by the very nature of
language; hence we cannot blame one for being incomplete, so
long as a subsequent page informs us that at a specific point of the
narrative something has been hidden from us (the first that

comes to mind—but that is merely the most striking among a thousand others—is that of *The Murder of Roger Ackroyd*, in which the narrator "neglects" to tell us that it is he who has committed the murder!). Ignorance and illusion therefore provoke two types of "correction" (only starting from which do they begin to exist): information in the narrow sense and reinterpretation of what we already knew—but imperfectly.

5. Lastly we may identify, within the perspective itself, a category somewhat apart, which is the *judgment* brought to bear on the events represented. The description of each part of the story can involve a moral evaluation; the absence of such judgment, moreover, constitutes a stand that is quite as significant. It is not necessary, for this judgment to affect us, that it be formulated explicitly: in order to realize the judgment brought to bear, we resort to a code of psychological principles and reactions that appear to be "natural." Just as the reader is not obliged to abide by an "outside" perspective but can deduce an entirely different "inside" one, here he may not accept the ethical and aesthetic judgments inherent in the perspective; the history of literature affords many examples of a reversal of values that causes us to admire the "bad" and to dismiss the "good" in a fiction sufficiently distant from us.

In the last three hundred years of fiction writing, one has become particularly aware of the effects that could be achieved by working and reworking the narrative perspective, and a series of writers, from Henry James to Faulkner, have exploited these possibilities rather feverishly. Nowadays, however, literature seems no longer to attach the same importance to this question. Perhaps the reason for this is that a certain tendency of modern writing does not propose to make us *see* anything whatever: it is discourse without being fiction. Here is the way a text without viewpoint is articulated:

"I seem to speak, it is not I, about me, it is not about me. These few general remarks to begin with. What am I to do, what shall I do, what should I do, in my situation, how proceed? By aporia pure and simple? Or by affirmations and negations invalidated as uttered, or sooner or later? Generally speaking. There must be other shifts. Otherwise it would be quite hopeless. But it is quite hopeless" (Beckett, *The Unnameable*).

In this discourse, which turns endlessly back on itself, which concerns nothing but itself, there is no longer any room for viewpoint. Its role is secured by the registers of speech: if in James the armature of a work was formed by the interplay of viewpoints, in Maurice Roche, for example, it is constituted by the particular arrangement of registers. We touch here upon a limit: that of the pertinence that the study of the text's verbal aspect can have, since this aspect is in a relation of solidarity with fiction itself.

All the categories of the verbal aspect hitherto examined might be considered from a different perspective, in which the discourse would no longer be put in relation with the fiction it creates, but the sum of the two would be put in relation with someone who assumes this discourse, the "subject of the speech-act" or, as we habitually say in literature, the *narrator.* This leads us to the problems of the narrative *voice.*

The narrator is the agent of all this labor of construction that we have just observed; consequently, all the latter's ingredients inform us indirectly about the former's nature. It is the narrator who incarnates the principles from which judgments of value are brought to bear; he conceals or reveals the characters' thoughts, thereby letting us participate in his conception of "psychology"; it is he who chooses between direct and transposed discourse, between chronological order and temporal disruptions.

Yet the degrees of the narrator's presence can also vary a great deal. Not only because his interventions, as we have just evoked them, can be more or less discreet; but because the narrative possesses an additional means of rendering the narrator present: making him figure within the fictive universe. The difference between the two cases is so great that on occasion two distinct terms have been used to characterize them, referring to a *narrator* with regard only to an explicit representation, and reserving the term *implied author* for the general case. It must not be supposed that the appearance of the first person ("I") suffices to distinguish one from the other: the narrator can say "I" without intervening in the fictive universe, by representing himself not as a character but as an author writing the book (the classic example is that of Diderot's *Jacques le Fataliste*).

There is sometimes a tendency to minimize the role of this opposition, because of a reductionist conception of language. Yet there is an impassable barrier between the narrative in which the narrator sees everything his character sees but does not appear on stage, and the narrative in which a character-narrator says "I." To confuse them would be to reduce language to zero. To see a house, and to say "I see a house," are two actions not only distinct but in opposition. Events can never "tell themselves": the act of verbalization is irreducible. Otherwise, we should confuse the "I" with the real subject of the speech-act, who recounts the book. Once the subject of the speech-act becomes the subject of the discourse, it is no longer the same subject who discourses. To speak of oneself signifies no longer being the same "oneself." The author is unnameable: if we want to give him a name, he leaves us the name but is not to be discovered behind it; he takes eternal refuge in anonymity. He is quite as fugitive as any subject of the speech-act, who by definition cannot be represented. In "He runs," there is "he," subject of the discourse, and "I," subject of the speech-act. In "I run," a spoken *subject of the speech-act* is intercalated between the two, taking from each a part of its preceding content but without making them disappear altogether: it merely hides them. For "he" and "I" still exist: this "I" who runs is not the same as the one who discourses. "I" does not reduce two to one, but out of two makes three.

The true narrator, the subject of the speech-act of the text in which a character says "I," is only the more disguised thereby. A narrative in the first person does not make the image of its narrator explicit, but on the contrary renders it still more implicit. And every effort at such explicitation can lead only to a more nearly perfect dissimulation of the subject of the speech-act; this discourse that acknowledges itself to be discourse merely conceals its property as discourse.

But it would be just as mistaken to detach this narrator altogether from the "implied author" and to regard him simply as one character among the rest. The comparison of narrative with drama may be illuminating here. In the case of drama, each character is (and is only) a source of words. But the difference between the two literary forms is deeper: in a narrative in which the narrator says "I," one character, among all the others, has a role apart; in the drama, all are on the same level. And this narrator-character is drawn differently from the others: if we can read both the remarks of the characters and their description by the narrator, the narrator does not *speak,* as do the protagonists of the narrative, he *recounts.* Hence, far from combining in himself the hero and the narrator, the person who "recounts" the book has a unique position: as different from the character he would have been if he were called "he," as from the narrator (implied author) who is a potential "I."

It must be added that this narrator-character can take a central role in the fiction (be the main character) or, on the contrary, be merely a discreet witness. One example of the first case, among many others: *Notes from Underground;* of the second, *The Brothers Karamazov.* Between the two occur countless intermediary cases where we shall find (to note only a few divergent examples) Zeitblom in *Doctor Faustus,* Tristam Shandy, as well as the famous Dr. Watson.

As soon as we identify the narrator (in the broad sense) of a book, we must also acknowledge the existence of his "partner," the one to whom the discourse uttered is addressed and whom we may call the *narratee.* The narratee is not the real reader, any more than the narrator is the author: we must not confuse the role with the actor who takes it. This simultaneous appearance is merely an instance of the general semiotic law according to which "I" and "you" (or rather: the sender and the receiver of a message) are always united. The functions of the narratee are many: "he constitutes," as Gerald Prince says, "a relay between narrator and reader; he helps specify the context of the narration, he serves to characterize the narrator, he puts certain themes in relief, he makes the plot advance, he becomes the mouthpiece of the work's ethic." Study of the narratee is as necessary to the knowledge of narration as that of the narrator.

v. The Syntactic Aspect: Structures of the Text

We shall now turn to the last group of problems of literary analysis, which we have grouped under the name of the syntactic aspect of the text. Here we postulate that every text can be decomposed into minimal units. The type of relations established between these copresent units will serve as a first criterion to distinguish several textual structures among them.

It is necessary to assert first, with a view to the distinctions that will follow, that it is virtually impossible to find these structures separated: a particular work uses several types of relation among its units at the same time, and therefore obeys several orders at once. If we say that a book illustrates this structure rather than that one, the reason is that the relation in question is predominant there. This notion of dominance or of *importance* has already appeared several times in the present study, but it is not yet possible for us to make it entirely explicit. We shall therefore confine ourselves to saying that this dominance has quantitative aspects (it designates the type of relation most frequent between units) as well as qualitative ones (these relations between units appear at privileged moments).

We shall distinguish two main types of organization of the text, thereby following a suggestion of Tomashevski: "We may distinguish two major kinds of arrangement of these thematic elements: (1) that in which causal-temporal relationships exist between the thematic elements, and (2) that in which the thematic elements are contemporaneous, or in which there is some shift of theme without internal exposition of the causal connections" (p. 66).

1. Logical and Temporal Order

Most works of fiction of the past are organized according to an order that we may qualify as both temporal and logical; let us add at once that the logical relation we habitually think of is implication, or as we ordinarily say, *causality.*

Causality is closely linked to temporality; it is even easy to confuse the two. Here is the way their difference is illustrated by E. M. Forster, who assumes that every novel possesses one and the other but that the former constitutes its plot, the second its story:

"'The king died and then the queen died' is a narrative. 'The king died, and then the queen died of grief' is a plot *(Aspects of the Novel).*

But if almost every causal narrative also possesses a temporal order, we only rarely manage to perceive the latter. The reason for this is a certain determinist state of mind, which we unconsciously attach to the very genre of narrative. "Indeed, there is a strong presumption that the mainspring of the narrative activity is to be traced to that very confusion between consecutiveness and consequence, what-comes-*after* being read in a narrative as what-is-*caused*-by. Narrative would then be a systematic application of the logical fallacy denounced by scholasticism under the formula *post hoc, ergo propter hoc.* . . ." writes Roland Barthes (p. 248). The logical series is in the reader's eyes a much stronger relation than the temporal series; if the two go together, he sees only the first.

It is possible to conceive of cases in which the logical and the temporal are to be found in the pure state, separated from each other; but we shall then be obliged to leave the field of what we habitually call literature. Pure chronological order, stripped of all causality, is dominant in chronicles, annals, diaries. Pure causality dominates axiomatic discourse (that of the logician) or teleological discourse (often that of the lawyer, of the political orator). In literature, we find a version of pure causality in the genre of the *portrait,* or in other descriptive genres, where the suspension of time is obligatory (a characteristic example: Kafka's tale *A Little Woman*). Sometimes, conversely, a "temporal" literature rejects, in appearance at least, submission to causality. Such works may assume quite explicitly the form of a chronicle or a "saga," like *Buddenbrooks.* But the most striking example of submission to the temporal order is *Ulysses.* The only, or at least the main, relation among the actions is their pure succession: we are told, minute after minute, what happens in a certain place or in the mind of the character. Digressions, as the classical novel experienced them, are no longer possible here, for they would indicate the existence of a structure other than temporal; the only form in which they can be admitted are the characters' dreams and memories.*

These exceptional cases merely emphasize the habitual solidarity between temporality and causality, in which the latter plays the dominant part. But causality, too, can be analyzed into several types. From our perspective, one opposition matters more than any other: do the minimal units of causality enter into an immediate relation with each other, or do they do so only by the intermediary of a general law of which they happen to be the illustrations? Given the use made of the one causality and the other, we shall designate a narrative in which the former causality predominates as *mythological* narrative, and the one in which the latter does as *ideological*.

(a). The narrative we are here calling *mythological* is the one that first provoked investigations of a "structuralist" inspiration. Utilizing the ideas of the Formalists, his contemporaries, Vladimir Propp published, in 1928, the first systematic study of this type of narrative. It is true that Propp was concerned with a unique genre, the fairy tale; and he studies it only in Russian examples; but the primary elements of any narrative of this type have been discerned in his work, and the many studies inspired by Propp habitually proceed in the direction of generalization. We shall return in greater detail to this type of narrative in subsequent chapters.

Immediate causality must not be reduced to the relation among *actions* alone (as Propp has a tendency to do): it is also possible that action provokes a state or is provoked by a state. This leads to narratives known as "psychological" (but we shall see that this

---

*This form of referential temporality is not the only one that narrative acknowledges. Alongside the temporality of discourse, there also exists a temporality of the speech-act, which is formed by the linking of "instances of discourse," i.e., of temporal coordinates that the discourse gives for its own speech-act; it is this very instance that defines the present tense as the tense of the speech-act; the work obeying this temporality is in an incessant present tense. We might call this second temporality the "time of writing," in opposition to the time represented. Sometimes the work is constituted by the explicit interplay of these two temporalities. Thus Michel Butor's *Passing Time*, in which the time of writing plays a greater and greater part, finally overwhelming the time represented in an ultimate coincidence of the two temporalities: the narrator no longer has time to tell the story.

term can cover very different realities). In his "Introduction to the Structural Analysis of Narrative," Barthes has shown how necessary it is to analyze the notion of causality: alongside the units which cause or are caused by similar units (which he calls "functions"), there exists another type of units, called "indices," which "instead of referring to a complementary and consequential act, refers to a more or less diffuse concept which is nonetheless necessary to the story: personality traits concerning the characters, information with regard to their identity, notations of 'atmosphere,' and so on" (p. 247).

(b). *Ideological* narrative establishes no direct relation between the units that constitute it; but these appear to our eyes as so many manifestations of one and the same idea, of a single law. It sometimes becomes necessary to carry abstraction quite far in order to find the relation between two actions whose copresence appears at first glance purely contingent.

Let us consider an example more closely: Constant's *Adolphe.* The rules that govern the characters' behavior are two, essentially. The first derives from the logic of desire as it is asserted by this book; we might formulate it thus: one desires what one does not have, one flees what one has. Consequently, obstacles reinforce desire, and cooperation weakens it. A first blow is administered to Adolphe's love when Ellénore leaves the Count de P*** in order to live with Adolphe. A second, when she dedicates herself to caring for him, after he is wounded. Each of Ellénore's sacrifices exasperates Adolphe: it leaves him even fewer things to desire. On the other hand, when Adolphe's father decides to provoke the couple's separation, the effect is the converse, and Adolphe expresses this explicitly: "Supposing you are separating me from her, you may well be attaching me to her forever." The tragic aspect of this situation derives from the fact that desire, in order to obey this particular logic, does not thereby cease to be desire: i.e., to cause the unhappiness of the one who cannot satisfy it.

The second law of this universe, also an ethical one, will be formulated as follows by Constant: "The great question in life is the pain one causes, and the most ingenious metaphysics does not justify the man who has broken the heart that loved him." One cannot order one's life by the search for the good, the happiness of one always being the misery of another. But one can organize it, starting with the demand that one do as little harm as possible: this negative value will be the only one to have an absolute status here. The commandments of this law will prevail over those of the first, when the two are in contradiction. This is what makes it so difficult for Adolphe to tell Ellénore the "truth." "In speaking thus, I saw her face suddenly covered with tears: I stopped, retraced my steps, denied, explained" (chapter 4). In chapter 6, Ellénore hears him to the end; she falls senseless, and Adolphe can only reassure her of his love. In chapter 8, he has an excuse for leaving her, but will not take advantage ot it: "Could I punish her for the imprudence I was making her commit, and in cold hypocrisy, seek a pretext in these very imprudences in order to abandon her without pity?" Pity prevails over desire.

Hence, certain isolated and independent actions, often performed by different characters, reveal the same abstract rule, the same ideological organization.

Twentieth-century literature has contributed serious correctives to the earlier images of causality. Very often, it has sought to escape causality's domination entirely; but even when it submits to that domination, it has transformed it considerably. On the one hand, since the end of the preceding century, writers have greatly diminished the absolute importance of the events described: whereas exploits, love, and death had once constituted the favored terrain of literature, Flaubert, Chekhov, and Joyce orient literature toward the insignificant and the everyday; and its causality resembles a parody of causality. On the other hand, a literature of initially fantastic inspiration has replaced the causality of common sense by a so to speak irrational causality; here we are in the realm of anti-causality, but this is still causality's realm. Such is the case for the narratives of Kafka or Gombrowicz and, in a different fashion, for the recent "literature of the absurd." A causality obviously very different from, say, Boccaccio's.

In dealing with causality, we must avoid reducing it to what might be called *explicit* causality. There is a difference between

"John throws a stone. The window breaks." and "The window breaks *because* John throws a stone." Causality is just as present in one case as in the other, but only in the second is it explicit. This distinction is often invoked in order to single out good or bad writers, the latter supposedly cultivating explicit causality; but this assertion seems unfounded. Hence it is said that popular or mass literature (whodunits, science fiction, spy stories) is characterized by its obvious and crude causality; but we have seen that Hammett is the very type of the writer who suppresses indications of a causal order.

If a narrative is organized according to a causal order but keeps its causality implicit, it thereby obliges the potential reader to perform labor the narrator has refused to do. Insofar as this causality is necessary for perception of the work, the reader must supply it; he then finds himself much more determined by the work than in the contrary case: it is actually up to him to reconstruct the narrative. We might say that every book requires a certain quantity of causality; the narrator and the reader supply it between them, their efforts being inversely proportional.

2. Spatial Order

Works organized according to this order are not habitually called "narrative"; the type of structure in question has been more widespread, in the past, in poetry than in prose. It is also within poetry that it has been chiefly studied. We may characterize this order, in a general way, as the existence of a certain more or less regular disposition of the units of the text. The logical or temporal relations shift to the background or disappear; it is the spatial relations of the elements that constitute the organization. (This "space" must obviously be taken in a particular sense, and designate a notion immanent to the text.)

The following poem by I. and P. Garnier illustrates a first variety of spatial structure:

    lyslyslyslyslys
    lyslyslyslyslys
    lyslyslyslyslys
    lyslyslyslyslys
    lyslyslyslyslys
    lyslyslyslyslys

This text, whose arrangement is formed by the order of the letters, is obviously no more than a rather naïve illustration of a fundamental principle of poetry. We may recall here all designs made with letters, whether we think of Mallarmé's *Un coup de dès* or again of Apollinaire's *Calligrammes*. More important are anagrams, texts in which certain letters form a word not only as given side by side, but also when removed from their place and reset in a different order. Such letters referring to letters, or sounds referring to sounds, create a space on the level of the signifier.

A systematic study of the spatial order in literature has been made by Roman Jakobson. In his analysis of poetry, he has shown that all the strata of discourse, from the phoneme and its distinctive features to grammatical categories and tropes, can enter into a complex organization, in symmetries, gradations, antitheses, parallelisms, etc., forming together a veritable spatial structure. Moreover, it is no accident that the discussion Jakobson devotes to parallelism is followed by a reference to geometry; nor that his most abstract formulation of the "poetic function" assumes this form: at every level of language, he would say, the essence of artistic technique in poetry resides in reiterated returns. What Jakobson would call "every level" nicely indicates the omnipresence of spatial relations: a whole narrative can similarly obey this spatial order, being based on symmetry, gradation, repetition, antithesis, etc. It is also a spatial comparison that Proust laid claim to in describing his work as a cathedral.

Today, literature is oriented toward narratives of a spatial and temporal type, to the detriment of causality. A book like Philippe Sollers's *Drame* combines these two orders in a complex interrelation emphasizing the time of writing and making two types of discourse alternate, led by an "I" and by a "he." Other works are organized around an alternation of verbal registers, or of grammatical categories, semantic networks, etc.

Only a *mixture* of such orders is actually encountered in literature. Pure causality refers us to utilitarian discourse, pure temporality to the elementary forms of history (science), pure spatiality to lettristic logatomy. May this not be one of the reasons for the difficulties we encounter when we attempt to speak of the structure of the text?

vi. The Syntactic Aspect: Narrative Syntax

In the next two chapters, we shall confine ourselves to a single kind of syntactic organization: the one that characterizes "mythological" narrative.

We have maintained from the start that our object here was constituted by the relations of narrative units among themselves. Now we must consider the nature of these units at closer range. We shall establish to this end three types of units, of which the first two are analytic constructions, while the third is given empirically: these are the *clause,* the *sequence,* and the *text* itself. We shall take as our example, in order to illustrate these notions, some tales from the *Decameron.*

1. The establishment of the smallest narrative unit is a problem that had already concerned one of the precursors of the Russian Formalists, the literary historian Alexander Vesselovski. To designate it, he uses the term *motif,* borrowed from the poetics of folklore, and gives it the following intuitive definition: "By motif, I mean the simplest narrative unit which corresponds, figuratively, to the various interrogrations of primitive mentality or the observation of manners." An example of motif would be: the dragon abducts the king's daughter. But Propp, while making use of Vesselovski's findings, already criticized this way of looking at things: such a sentence is not yet an entity that cannot be decomposed: it contains no fewer than four elements: the dragon, the abduction, the daughter, the king! To mitigate this disadvantage, Propp introduces an additional selective criterion, which is constancy/variability; he perceives, for instance, that in the Russian fairy tale the stable element is the abduction, whereas the other three vary from one tale to the next; and he declares that only the former deserves the name of *function,* which becomes his fundamental unit.

But by introducing the criterion of constancy/variability, Propp is obliged to leave general poetics behind and to enter that of a particular genre (the fairy tale, in Russia to boot); we may readily conceive another genre in which the constant element would be the king, the other "motifs" being variables. In order to avoid Propp's criticism of Vesselovski, though without committing ourselves to a "generic" poetics, the best solution would be to reduce the initial "motif" to a series of elementary propositions, in the logical sense of the term; for example:

> X is a young girl
> Y is a king
> Y is X's father
> Z is a dragon
> Z abducts X

We shall call this minimal unit the *narrative proposition.* The proposition involves, it would appear, two kinds of constituents, which we may call respectively agents (X, Y, Z) and *predicates* (to abduct, to be a young girl, a dragon, etc.)

The agents are two-sided units. On the one hand, they permit us to identify discontinuous elements located in space and time; this is a *referential* function that is assumed, in ordinary speech, by proper nouns (as well as by those expressions accompanied by a demonstrative): we might substitute, without changing anything in the preceding presentation, "Mary" for X, "John" for Y, etc.; this is what happens in real narratives, where the agents generally correspond to individual beings and, what is more, to humans. On the other hand, the agents occupy a certain position in relation to the verb: for example, in the last proposition above, Z is a subject, X is an object. This is the *syntactic* function of the agents, which from this point of view are no different from the syntactic functions proper to language, and which are expressed in many languages in the form of cases (hence the origin of the term "agent"). According to the investigations of Claude Bremond, these main roles are agent and patient, each specified according to several parameters: the first as influencer and ameliorator (or corruptor), the second as beneficiary and victim.

The predicates can be of all sorts, for they correspond to the entire variety of the lexicon; but there has long been an agreement to identify two major classes of predicates, by selecting as discriminative criterion the predicate's relation with the preceding one. Tomashevski has formulated this distinction, which in his vocabulary is applied to motifs: "A story may be thought of as a journey from one situation to another. . . . Motifs which change the situation are *dynamic motifs;* those which do not are *static"* (p. 70). This dichotomy makes explicit the grammatical distinction between adjective and verb (the substantive being assimilated here to the adjective). Let us add that the adjectival predicate is given as anterior to the process of denomination, whereas the verbal predicate is contemporary with this same process; as Sapir says, the first is an "existant," the second an "occurrant."

Let us take an example from the *Decameron* that will allow us to illustrate these "parts" of narrative discourse. Peronella receives her lover in the absence of her husband, a poor mason. But one day the husband returns early. Peronella hides the lover in a cask; once the husband is in the house, she tells him that someone wanted to buy the cask and that this someone is now in the process of examining it. The husband believes her and rejoices over the sale. He will scrape out the cask to clean it; meanwhile the lover, who has left the cask, makes love to Peronella, who has leaned over the opening of the cask, thereby blocking the view of the husband, inside it, as to what is happening outside.

Peronella, the lover, and the husband are the agents of this story; we may designate them by X, Y, and Z. The words lover and husband further indicate a certain condition (the legality of the relationship with Peronella, here in question); they therefore function as adjectives. These adjectives describe the initial condition: Peronella is the mason's wife, she is not entitled to make love with other men.

Then comes the transgression of this law: Peronella receives her lover. Here we are dealing with a "verb," obviously, which we may designate as: to violate, to transgress (a law). It brings about a state of disequilibrium, for the family law is no longer respected.

From this moment, two possibilities exist in order to re-establish equilibrium. The first would be to punish the unfaithful wife; but this action would have served to re-establish the *initial* equilibrium. Now, the tale (or at least, Boccaccio's tales) never describes such a repetition of the initial order. The verb "to punish" is therefore presented within the tale (it is the danger that threatens Peronella) but it is not realized, it remains in a virtual state. The second possibility consists in finding a means of evading punishment; this is what Peronella does; she succeeds by disguising the situation of disequilibrium (the transgression of the law) as a situation of equilibrium (the purchase of a cask does not violate the family law). Hence there is a new verb here, "to disguise." The final result is again a state, hence an adjective: a new law is established, though it is not explicit, according to which the wife can follow her natural inclinations.

2. Having thus given a description of the minimal unit that is the proposition, we can return to our initial question, bearing on the *relations* between minimal units. We can say at once that, from the point of view of their content, these relations are distributed among the different "orders" of causality or of inclusion; temporal relations, of succession or of simultaneity; "spatial" relations, of repetition, opposition, and so on. But the combination of the propositions presents other special features.

First of all, the establishment of a higher unit is necessary. The propositions do not form infinite chains, they are organized into cycles that every reader recognizes intuitively (one has the impression of a completed whole) and that analysis identifies without too much difficulty. This higher unit is called *sequence;* the limit of the sequence is marked by an incomplete repetition (we should prefer to say: a transformation) of the initial proposition. If, for convenience's sake, we admit that this initial proposition describes a stable state, it follows that the complete sequence is composed — always and only — of five propositions. An ideal narrative begins with a stable situation that some force will perturb. From which results a state of disequilibrium; by the action of a force directed in a converse direction, the equilibrium is re-established; the second equilibrium is quite similar to the first, but the two are not identical. Consequently there are two types of episodes in a narrative: those that describe a state (of equilibrium or of disequilibrium) and those that describe the transition from one state to the other. In this description we may recognize attributive and verbal propositions. It is of course possible that the sequence will be cut in the middle (transition from equilibrium to disequilibrium alone, or conversely), or even into still smaller parts.

The formula "transition from one state to the other" (or as Tomashevski says, "from one situation to another") deals with phenomena on the most abstract level. But this "transition" or passage can be realized by different means. It is to the study of the ramification of the abstract initial schema that Claude Bremond has devoted his *Logique de récit*, in which he attempts to draw up a systematic chart of all "narrative possibilities."

The sequence as we have defined it involves a minimal number of propositions; but it can include more without our thereby being able to identify two autonomous sequences: this is due to the fact that not all the propositions enter into the basic schema. Here again, Tomashevski has proposed a first distinction (by applying it, again, to "motifs," which therefore, in his work, cover *both* the predicates and the propositions): "The motifs of a work are heterogeneous. A simple account of the fable shows that certain motifs can be omitted without thereby destroying the succession of the narrative whereas others cannot be omitted without affecting the link of causality that unites events. The motifs that cannot be excluded are called *associated motifs;* those that can be set aside without damaging the chronological and causal succession of events are called *free motifs.*" Here we may recognize the opposition Barthes formulates between "functions" and "indices." It follows that these optional ("free") propositions (or "indices") are such only from the point of view of sequential construction; they are often what is most necessary in the text as a whole.

3. What the reader encounters empirically is neither the proposition nor the sequence, but an entire *text:* a novel, a tale, a play. Now, a text almost always includes more than one sequence. Three types of combinations among sequences are possible.

The first case, frequent in the *Decameron,* is embedding. Here an entire sequence is substituted for a proposition of the first sequence. For example:

Bergamin arrives in a foreign city, invited to a feast by Messire Cane; at the last moment, the latter cancels the invitation without compensating Bergamin, who finds himself obliged to spend a good deal of money; but happening to meet Messire Cane one day day, he tells him the story of Primas and the Abbé of Cluny. Primas had attended a banquet given by the abbé without being invited to it, and the abbé had refused to give him any food. Later on, overtaken by remorse, the abbé loaded Primas with gifts. Messire

Cane understands the allusion and causes Bergamin to be reimbursed.

The main sequence includes all its obligatory elements: Bergamin's initial state, its degeneration, the state of distress in which he finds himself, the means he discovers to emerge from it, his final state similar to the first one. But the fourth proposition is a narrative which forms a sequence in its turn: this is the technique of embedding.

There are several varieties of embedding, depending on the narrative level of the two sequences (the same level or a different level, as in the case cited) and on the type of thematic relation established between them: a relation of causal explanation; a relation of thematic juxtaposition, as with arguments or examples or stories that form a contrast with the preceding one; finally, as Shklovski remarks, we can "tell stories in order to delay the performance of some action"; the example of Scheherazade immediately comes to mind.

Linking affords another possibility of combination. In this case case, the sequences are put one after the other instead of being embedded one within the other. Hence in the seventh tale of the eighth day: Helena leaves the amorous clerk in the garden for a whole cold winter night (first sequence), then the clerk shuts her up naked in a tower for a whole hot summer day (second sequence). The two sequences have identical structures: the identity is emphasized by the opposition of spatio-temporal circumstances. Linking also includes several semantic and syntactic subspecies; Shklovski for example distinguished "stringing together," in which the same protagonist passes through various adventures (the *Gil Blas* type), "step-construction" or parallelism of sequences, etc.

The third form of combination is *alternation* (or *interlacing*), which places a proposition of the first sequence before or after one of the second. The *Decameron* offers few examples of this type (though there is the first story of the Fifth Day); but the novel frequently makes use of this construction. Hence in *Les Liaisons dangereuses* the stories of Madame de Tourvel and of Cecile alternate; alternation is motivated by the epistolary form of the book. These three elementary forms can, of course, be further combined among themselves.

vii. The Syntactic Aspect: Specifications and Reactions

After this general view, we must return to certain aspects of the narrative predicates hitherto passed over in silence.

1. Our preceding description might suggest that each predicate is absolutely different from all others. Now, even a superficial consideration permits us to note the relationship of certain actions, and hence the possibility of presenting them as *one* action possessing several forms. Propp had made a first effort in this direction by reducing all fairy tales to only thirty-one "functions." However, the apparently arbitrary choice of this figure has not convinced his readers: it is both too great and too small. Too small, if we think that all possible actions can be reduced by empirical regroupings to only thirty-one; too great, if we start not from the variety of actions but from an axiomatic model. Hence it has become a commonplace of Propp-criticism to indicate the possibility of combining several functions into one, while preserving their differences; for example, Lévi-Strauss writes: "We might regard 'violation' as the converse of 'prohibition', and the latter as a negative transformation of 'injunction'."

In language, those categories that permit both specification of an action and indication of the features it shares with others, are expressed by verbal terminations, by adverbs or particles. The simplest and most widespread example is *negation* (with its variant *opposition*). Bergamin is rich, then poor, then rich again: the important thing is to see that there are not two autonomous predicates here but two forms of the same predicate, positive and negative.

Negation appertains to what we call the "status" of the verb. Another verbal category is *aspect:* thus an action can be presented at its inception in the process of its performance, and as a conclusion (in grammar we call these aspects: inchoative, progressive, terminative). Even more important for narration is the category of *modality:* we have already observed an example of this in the story of Peronella, where the ban against adultery played an essential part; now, what is a ban if not a proposition of negative status, expressed in the mode of obligation ("Thou shalt not . . .")?

This type of *specification* seems obvious enough when it is inscribed within the grammar of the language; but we must be aware of the fact that any adverb of manner can play an analogous part. We can characterize all kinds of actions as being "well" or "badly" performed, thereby establishing their common features; and conversely, we can specify one and the same action depending on whether it is performed in this or that manner.

This kind of logical analysis (rather than grammatical, despite how it may strike us at first glance) is not a simple artifice of notation; it permits us to extend analysis to its irreducible units, which is a necessary condition of any exigent description.

2. It is apparent that in the case of predicates we must proceed to that regrouping and classification that lead to the establishment of categories serving to modify (or to specify) the initial predicate. There exists another way of regrouping the primary or secondary nature.

There are, as a matter of fact, primary actions that do not presuppose the accomplishment of any other action. For example, to return to a case already considered, we may learn that the dragon abducts Mary without knowing that Mary is a king's daughter: such propositions follow each other, sometimes causally linked, but nothing keeps them from also existing in isolation. The case is quite otherwise with an action such as, precisely, *learning.* Let us imagine that Ivan learns of Mary's abduction. Such an action will be called secondary, for it presupposes the existence of an anterior proposition, which is: someone abducts Mary. Forcing somewhat the meaning of the words, we might speak in the first case of *actions,* in the second, of *reactions:* reactions always and necessarily appear following another action.

Can we give a descriptive list of all reactions? Actually we have already done so once, and it is no accident if in the preceding paragraph the word "learn" has appeared twice, once with "we" as its subject and then with "Ivan" (the character). Just as we engage in an effort to construct fiction starting from a discourse, in exactly the same way the characters, elements of the fiction, must reconstitute their universe starting from the discourse and signs that surround them. Thus every fiction contains within itself a representation of this same process of reading to which we submit it.

The characters construct their reality starting from the signs they receive, just as we construct the fiction starting from the text read; their apprenticeship to the world is an image of ours to the book.

Hence we shall recognize here all the categories we had established in our description of the "verbal aspect" of the literary work; and we may make use of them in order to focus our typology of narrative predicates. Let us take the example of *time*. Just as we readers can learn of an action before or after the moment it has, fictively, occurred (prospections and retrospections), similarly the characters are not content to experience an action but can also *remember* or *project* it as "reactions" that can exist only, so to speak, on the back of another action. Moreover, there exist many predicates linked to this interplay with time, according to their relation with the subject speaking, the degree of approbation given the action envisaged, etc. For instance, *to project* or *to decide* are actions assumed by this subject and refer only to him; *to promise* or *to threaten,* on the other hand, also concern the person to whom one speaks, and in actions such as *to hope* or *to fear,* the outcome of events does not depend on the subject.

We shall recognize the categories of *mode* if we turn to the problem of the transmission of information within fiction: here things can be *recounted* or *spoken* or *represented* with more or less fidelity, more or less distance (and, in the fictive universe, the act of recounting a thing, which is a "reaction," can have more narrative importance than the act of experiencing it).

But the most varied and most numerous reactions are connected to the different categories that we have identified within *perspective.*

The simplest case is that of *illusion*, or false information, and of its elimination. We recall Peronella's clever action, which *disguised* the situation of adultery into a situation of cask-purchase. Classical poetics has inventoried the complementary action of reinterpretation, or discovery of the truth (one of its versions, at least), under the name of *recognition*. Here is the Aristotelian formulation: "Recognition, as the name indicates moreover, is a passage from ignorance to knowledge . . . ." Recognition corresponds to two parts of the plot: first, a moment of "ignorance," later, that of "knowledge." In these two moments—for us, these two propositions—it is the same phenomenon that is evoked; but the first time someone has erred in interpretation, which makes it into a secondary action, or reaction. The most frequent examples concern the identity of a character: the first time, Iphegenia takes Orestes for someone else; the second time, she identifies him. But we see that it is not necessary to reduce recognition to the discovery of a real identity: any revelation concerning an action of which one has first given a false interpretation equals a "recognition." The case is not very different with *ignorance,* which implies a "reaction" of *apprenticeship.*

In saying that a character could "fear" or "hope for" the occurrence of an event, we were concerned only with the temporal value of these reactions; yet they also imply, of course, a value judgment—which can of course assume other forms than "good" and "bad." Finally, the simple fact of transposing an action from its objective state into the subjectivity of a character is equivalent to the existence of a perspective. "Peronella deceives her husband" is an action, "The husband thinks Peronella is deceiving him," a reaction (though one that does not occur in Boccaccio's tale).

Hence everything that might seem a simple process of presentation on the level of discourse is transformed into a thematic element on the level of fiction.

It is important to see the difference between specifications and reactions: in the former case, it was a matter of the various forms of one and the same predicate; in the latter, of two types of different predicates, primary and secondary, or actions and reactions. The presence and the position of this or that type of predicate strongly influence our perception of a text. What is more striking in a narrative like the *Quest for the Grail* than these two "reactions": on the one hand, all events are announced in advance; on the other, once they have happened, they receive a new interpretation in a particular symbolic code.

Literature at the end of the nineteenth century particularly favored the representation of the process of learning; the method reaches its apotheosis in the work of a Henry James or a Barbey d'Aurevilly, where we are often told *only* the apprenticeship process without ever learning anything at all: either because there is nothing to learn or because the truth is unknowable. Such texts achieve to a particularly powerful degree that position *"en abyme"* that is the estate of all literature: the book, like the world, must be *interpreted.*

Chapter Three
Perspectives

i. Poetics and Literary History

From the beginning, we have noticed the relation of complementarity between poetics and criticism; now that we have completed this schematic description of the literary work, we can attempt to compare poetics with the other disciplines that traditionally participate in the field of literature.

And first of all, with *literary history.* But before undertaking such a comparison, we must look more closely at what is designnated by these two words. Denouncing the ambiguity of the term, Tynianov wrote in 1921: "Meanwhile, the historical investigations of literature fall into at least two main types, depending on the points of observation: the investigation of the genesis of literary phenomena, and the investigation of the evolution of a literary order, that is, of literary changeability. The point of view determines not only the significance but also the nature of the phenomenon studied" (p. 67). We shall start from this opposition, though giving it a different meaning from Tynianov's.

The *genesis* of the work was regarded by the Formalists as exterior to literature, as functioning according to a relation between the literary "series" and some other "series." But such an assertion comes up against two objections that, oddly, were also initially formulated by this same Tynianov. In the study of the "Theory of

Parody," he had shown the impossibility of wholly understanding a text by Dostoevsky without reference to a certain earlier text of Gogol. It was after this work that investigations began into what we have called the polyvalent (or dialogic) register. From which we learn that genesis is inseparable from structure, the story from the creation of the book, of its meaning: if we were ignorant of the parodic function of the Dostoevskian text (at first glance, a simple element of its genesis), our comprehension of it would suffer seriously.

In another study, written some years later and bearing on "the literary fact," Tynianov showed the impossibility of giving this latter notion an atemporal, ahistorical definition: a certain kind of writing (for example the diary) will be regarded at one period as belonging to literature and as external to it at another. Behind this acknowledgment of impotence another thesis was being asserted (though one Tynianov did not formulate), according to which certain nonliterary texts could play a decisive part in the formation of a literary work.

If we bring together these two separate conclusions, we must apparently revise the initial judgment that regarded genesis as an external phenomenon, worthy of the interest of psychologists and sociologists, but not of the literary critic. As far back as we trace genesis, we find only other texts, other products of language; and it is difficult for us to conceive their apportionment. Must we exclude from the linguistic factors that preside over the genesis of a novel by Balzac the writings of those who were not poets but philosophers, moralists, memorialists, chroniclers of social life? Or even that anonymous but insistent text that fills newspapers, lawbooks, everyday conversation? The same is true for the relation between the various works of an author. We are in agreement today in considering as "relevant" the relation between two poems by the same writer; but can we exclude the relation between this same poem and the perhaps contradictory evocation of its theme, of its lexicon, in a letter to a friend (simply because the letter is not "literature")?

We cannot conceive the "outside," the "exterior" of language and of the symbolic. Life is a bio-graphy, the world a socio-graph, and we never reach an "extra-symbolic" or "pre-linguistic" state.

Genesis, too, is not "extra-literary", but it must be admitted that at present the very term is no longer appropriate: there is no genesis of texts starting from what is not the texts themselves, but always and only a work of *transformation,* from one discourse into another, from the text to the text.

The difference between genesis and variability is therefore not in the degree of their "interiority" to literature. It is, on the other hand, parallel to another already established distinction, which is that between criticism (or interpretation) and poetics. For it is not works that vary, it would appear, but literature; conversely, it is exclusively with works that we are concerned when we speak, as above, of genesis.*

The study of variability, then, is an integral part of poetics, since it concerns, like the latter, the abstract categories of literary discourse, and not individual works. In this perspective, we can envisage studies bearing on each of the concepts of poetics. We shall describe the development of psychological causality in plot, or the evolution of the registers of discourse and their use in literature. Such studies, evidently, will not be qualitatively different from those we have found inscribed within the field of poetics. At the same time, the factitious opposition between "structure" and "history" vanishes: it is only on the level of structures that we can describe literary development; not only does the knowledge of structures not impede that of variability, but indeed it is the sole means we possess of approaching the latter.

Here the notion of *genre* reappears. Like the concept of literary history, the concept of genre must be subjected first to a critical scrutiny. As a matter of fact, the word applies to two distinct realities for which Lämmert, in his study of 1955, reserves the terms *type,* on the one hand, and *genre* (in the narrow sense) on the other.

---

*We can also think of the genesis of literature, or of literary forms: this is the thesis of Andre Jolles's work of 1930, *Simple Forms;* for this author, who defines himself as a representative of the "morphological" tendency, the literary forms found in contemporary works are derived from linguistic forms; this derivation occurs not directly but by the intermediary of a series of "simple forms" that we find, for the most part, in folklore. Hence these simple forms are extensions and applications of linguistic forms; and they themselves will subsequently be taken as basic elements in the works of "high" literature. But the word genesis obviously assumes a different meaning here.

The type is defined as the conjunction of several properties of literary discourse, judged important for the works in which they are found. The type does not present any reality outside of theoretical reflection; it always supposes that we set aside several divergent features, judged unimportant, in favor of other—identical—features that are dominant in the work's structure. If there are only divergent features, each work represents a particular type; if there are divergent features, we regard all works as belonging to the same type (which is literature). Between these two poles are situated the types to which classical poetics has accustomed us, such as poetry and prose, tragedy and comedy, etc.

The type belongs to the object of general poetics, not of historical poetics.

This is not the case with genre, in the narrow sense. In every period, a certain number of literary types becomes so familiar to the public that the public uses them as keys (in the musical sense) for the interpretation of works; here the genre becomes, according to an expression of Hans Robert Jauss, a "horizon of expectation." The writer in his turn internalizes this expectation; the genre becomes for him a "model of writing." In other words, the genre is a type that has had a concrete historical existence, that has participated in the literary system of a period.

An example will permit us to illustrate these notions. We shall take it from Bakhtin's book on Dostoevsky's poetics. Bakhtin isolates a type with which we have rarely been concerned; he gives it the name of polyphonic or dialogic narrative (we shall return to his definition). This abstract type has been realized on several occasions, down through history, in concrete genres. Thus: in the Socratic dialogues, in Menippean satire of Latin literature, in "carnival" or festal literature of the Middle Ages and the Renaissance.

If then a first task of literary history is to study the variability of each literary category, the next step will be to consider the genres, both diachronically, as Bakhtin does (in other words, by studying the generic variants of a single type) and synchronically, in the relations of the genres among themselves. At the same time, we must not forget that in each period, the core of identical features is accompanied by a high number of other features that we nonetheless regard as less important and hence not decisive, in order to attribute a certain work to another genre. Consequently, a work is susceptible of belonging to different genres, depending on whether or not we judge a certain feature of its structure to be important. Hence for the Ancients, the *Odyssey* indisputably belonged to the genre "epic"; but for us this notion has lost its currency, and we should be rather inclined to attach the *Odyssey* to the genre "narrative" or even "mythological narrative."

A third task of literary history would be the identification of the *laws* of variability, which concern the transition of one literary "epoch" to another (supposing that such laws exist). Several models have been proposed that would permit us to render history's detours intelligible; there seems to have been a transition, in the history of poetics, between an "organic" model (a literary form is born, develops, and dies) to a "dialectical" model (thesis-antithesis-synthesis). We shall avoid concerning ourselves with such models here, but we must not thereby assume the nonexistence of the problem. Let us say that it is difficult to deal with it for the moment, in the absence of distinct works that would prepare the ground: having sought for so long to absorb the neighboring disciplines, literary history today figures as a poor relation: historical poetics is the least elaborated sector of poetics.

ii. Poetics and Aesthetics

Any literary analysis, whether or not it is structural, very often provokes this demand: to be judged satisfactory, it must be able to explain a work's aesthetic value, to say why, in other words, we judge one work to be beautiful and not another. And we suppose we have proved the failure of the analysis if it does not manage to give a satisfactory answer to this question. "Your theory is very pretty," we are told, "but what use is it to me, if it cannot explain the reasons why humanity has preserved and praised precisely the words that constitute the object of your studies?"

Critics have not remained insensitive to this reproach, and they have regularly attempted to answer it, to furnish a formula that, automatically applied, would produce beauty. It is scarcely necessary to remark that such formulas have always been violently attacked by the critics of the following generation, and that today we do not even remember all the attempts made to grasp beauty in a universal imperative. Let us cite, without comment, just one, which at least deserves attention because of its author: Hegel, who writes in the *Idea of the Beautiful:* "Just as the most ideal state of the world is compatible with specific periods in perference to others, art selects, for the figures which it situates, a specific milieu in preference to others: that of *princes.* And this not out of aristocratic sentiment or love of distinction; but it manifests thereby the freedom of the will and of creation, which manage to realize themselves only in the representation of princely environments."

The advent of poetics has revived the fateful question of the work's value. As soon as we try, by means of its categories, to describe a work's structure with some precision, we meet with the same mistrust as to the possibilities of explaining its beauty. We describe, for example, a poem's grammatical structures, or its phonic organization: but to what end? Does such a description allow us to understand why this poem is considered to be beautiful? And thereby the entire enterprise of a rigorous poetics is jeopardized.

Not that those who have identified and described certain important aspects of the work have not wanted to deal with the laws of beauty. There even exists such a law, formulated some fifty years ago apropos of the novel, that is still, even today, even in the most serious works, presented as a formula for beauty and quality. It deserves closer consideration.

The law concerns what was designated above as perspectives in narrative. When Henry James made these the basis of his literary and aesthetic program, readers had the impression of grasping, for the first time, a stable, apprehensible element of the work, one that might permit them to open the sesame of literary aesthetics. In his already cited book, Percy Lubbock attempted to judge the works of the past by a criterion derived from the knowledge of points of view: for the work to be successful, to be "beautiful," the narrator must not change point of view throughout the story; if there is a change, it must be justified by the plot and by the work's entire structure. By adopting such a criterion, a critic would inevitably set James's own works above those of Tolstoy.

This conception, still promulgated, has had curious extensions, without our being able to assert that its various partisans have influenced each other. Thus many of Bakhtin's affirmations can be located in this very perspective; in his book on Dostoevsky, certainly one of the most important in the realm of poetics, Bakhtin sets the dialogic or polyphonic "genre" in opposition to the monologic "genre" from which the traditional novel derives (we have seen that these were actually types). The dialogic is characterized, essentially, by the absence of a unifying narrative consciousness that would contain the consciousness of all the characters. In Dostoevsky's novels, which are the most accomplished examples of the dialogic, there does not exist, Bakhtin asserts, a narrator's consciousness isolated from the others on a higher level, which would assume the discourse of the whole. "The author's new position *vis-à-vis* the character in Dostoevsky's polyphonic novel consists in the dialogic position, rigorously respected, which affirms the independence, the inner freedom, the indetermination and the independence of the character. For the author, the character is not a 'he' nor an 'I' but a 'thou,' in the full sense of the second person singular, which is to say, a different 'I,' other but equal."

But Bakhtin does not stop with this description, which would entitle other works not to obey these laws without being thereby condemned: his entire analysis implies the superiority of this form over all others. For example, he writes:

The new artistic position of the author vis-à-vis the hero in Dostoevsky's polyphonic novel is a *consequent and fully realized dialogical position* which confirms the hero's independence, inner freedom, unfinalizedness and indeterminacy. For the author the hero is not "he" and not "I," but a full-valued "thou," that is, another full-fledged "I" ("Thou art") (p. 51).

The genuine life of the personality can be penetrated only *dialogically*, and then only when it mutually and voluntarily opens *itself* (p. 48).

Thus Bakhtin offers a different version of the aesthetic law established by Lubbock, following James. He specifies that viewpoint must correspond to what Pouillon calls viewpoint "with," and that there must be several of these within one and the same work. It is only on such conditions that the dialogue can be established.

We do not feel entitled to contest these conclusions so long as the example chosen remains Dostoevsky. Yet a few pages further, Bakhtin himself instances another case, that of an uncompleted work, in which the same dialogic principle happens to be illustrated. The author of this work is no longer Dostoevsky but Chernyshevsky, whose works have, to say the least, a fiercely debated aesthetic value. Once the dialogic principles leaves Dostoevsky's works, it loses its vaunted qualities.

Closer to us, Sartre has given a new formulation of Lubbock's law, in a famous essay on Mauriac. Mauriac's work is here contested not in the name of the aesthetic of the Sartian novel, but of the novel in general. Once again, the demand is for a vision, a viewpoint "with" (a single internal focusing) throughout the book.

There is no more place for a privileged observer in a real novel than in the world of Einstein. . . . But novels are written *by* men and *for* men. In the eyes of God, who cuts through appearances and goes beyond them, there is no novel, no art, for art thrives on appearances (p. 23).

Fictional beings have their laws, the most rigorous of which is the following: the novelist may be either their witness or their accomplice, but never both at the same time. The novelist must be either inside or out (p. 16).

What is the demand of this very special aesthetic? What it particularly condemns is the inequality of the two voices, that of the subject of the speech-act (the narrator) and that of the subject of the discourse (the character). If the former wants to be heard, he must disguise himself, assume the mask of the latter. Thus for Sartre: "Fictional beings have their laws, of which this is the most rigorous: the novelist can be their witness or their accomplice, but never both at once. Outside or inside." We cannot be both the same and other. The voices of two characters produce a polyphony; but it would appear that those of a character and a narrator who does not choose to conceal his quality as unique subject of the speech-act, can produce only a cacophony. The kind of cacophony of which the *Odyssey* and *Don Quixote* are examples.

Just as Bakhtin had used the example of Dostoevsky in his demonstration, Sartre, in his counter-demonstration, had used Mauriac. But we do not enunciate general truths on the showing of a single example. Let us take these sentences by Kafka:

"K at first was glad to be out of that overheated room where the maids and messengers were crowded together. It was a little cold outside, the snow had hardened, it was easier to walk now. Unfortunately it was beginning to grow dark, and K walked faster" *(The Castle).*

We are clearly being offered here the viewpoint "with." We follow K, we see and hear what he sees and hears, we know his thoughts but not those of others. And yet. . . . Let us take the two words "glad," "unfortunately". . . . The first time, K may feel glad, but he does not think: "I am glad." We are being given a description, not a quotation. It is K who feels glad, but it is someone else who writes: "K felt glad." This is no longer the case with "unfortunately." This word reflects an observation that K himself articulates; it is in consequence of this observation, and not because "it was beginning to grow dark" that he walks faster. In the first case, there is K's nameless sentiment and its denomination by the narrator. In the second case, it is K who verbalizes his own sentiment, and the narrator *transcribes* K's words instead of *describing* his sentiments: there is an obvious "modal" difference here.

In other words, the Lubbock-Bakhtin-Sartre law is not followed. There are two consciousnesses at once, and they are not on equal footing; the narrator remains a narrator, he cannot be identified with one of the characters. But how does this phenomenon destroy or harm the aesthetic value of the passage quoted? Might there not be, on the contrary, quite as much reason to assert that the imperceptible oscillation between the two subjects in a speech-act is one of the obligatory features of that ambiguous and uncertain perception that the reading of a masterpiece affords?

There is no question, of course, of substituting its opposite for this first law. What the preceding remarks aim at illustrating is the impossibility of formulating universal aesthetic laws from the analysis, however brilliant, of one or even of several works. All that we have been offered, till now, as recipes for value has been, in the best of cases, only a good description; and we must not present a description, even when it is a correct one, as an explanation of beauty. There exists no literary method whose use obligatorily produces an aesthetic experience.

What are we to do? Abandon all hope of ever discussing value? Trace an impassable limit between poetics and aesthetics, between a work's structure and its value? Leave the judgment of value to the members of literary juries?

The failure of the preceding attempts might readily lead us down this path. Yet it has only a relative importance. Poetics is still in its early stages. It is not surprising that, with the first labors, we should have raised questions concerning value; but it is also not surprising that the answers given should be unsatisfactory. For, suggestive as are the descriptions that these labors contain, they are only an initial and crude approximation, whose merit is rather to indicate a way to be taken. The problem of value seems more complex; and to answer the critics who reproach the analyses based on the principles of poetics for their nonpertinence with regard to the analysis of beauty, we might say, quite simply, that this question should be raised only much later on, that we must not begin at the end, before even the first steps have been taken. But we may also wonder in what direction our efforts should proceed.

It is an incontestable truth today that the value judgment of a work depends on the work's structure. But perhaps we must emphasize another phenomenon: structure is not the unique factor of judgment. We may suppose that in order to understand a work's value, we must abandon this first territorial division, necessary but impoverishing, which cuts the work off from its *reader*. The value is internal to the work, but it appears only at the moment when the work is interrogated by a reader. The reading is not only an act of the work's manifestation, but also a process of valorization. This hypothesis does not come down to asserting that a work's beauty is afforded solely by the reader, and that this process remains an individual experience impossible to define with any rigor; the value judgment is not a simple subjective judgment; but we would pass beyond this very limit between work and reader, and regard them as forming a dynamic unit.

Aesthetic judgments are propositions that strongly imply their own processes of utterance. We cannot conceive of such a judgment outside the instance of discourse in which it is made, nor in isolation from the subject articulating it. I can speak of the beauty that Goethe's works have for me; at the limit I can speak of the beauty they have for Schiller or Thomas Mann. But a question bearing on their beauty in itself has no meaning. It is perhaps to this property of aesthetic judgments that classical aesthetics referred when it asserted that such judgments are always individual, always particular.

We see clearly, in this perspective, why poetics cannot and indeed must not assign itself as an initial task the explication of aesthetic judgment. Such judgment presupposes not only the knowledge of the work's structure, which poetics must facilitate, but also a knowledge of the reader and of what determines his judgment. If this second part of the task is not unrealizable, if we find means to study what is commonly called the "taste" or the "sensibility" of a period, whether by investigation of the traditions forming them or of the aptitudes innate in each individual, then a passage will be established between poetics and aesthetics, and the old question as to the beauty of the work can be raised once again.

iii. Poetics as Transition

We began by saying that poetics is to be defined as a science of literature, in opposition both to interpretation of individual works (which deals with literature but does not constitute a science) and to the other sciences, such as psychology or sociology, in that it institutes literature itself as an object of knowledge, whereas previously literature was considered as one manifestation among others of the psyche or of society.

The constitutive gesture of poetics is irreproachable, since it annexes to the field of knowledge what had hitherto served merely as a means of access for knowledge of a different object.

However, this gesture turns out to have many implications that have been noted long ago. Instituting poetics as an autonomous discipline of which literature as such is the object, we postulate the autonomy of this object: if that were not sufficient, it would not permit us to establish the specificity of poetics. In 1919 Jakobson produced this formulation, which has since become famous: "The object of literary science is not literature but literariness, which is to say, what makes a given work a literary work." It is the specifically literary aspects of literature, those it alone possesses, that form the object of poetics. The autonomy of poetics is dependent upon that of literature.

It appears, in other words, that the recognition of literature as an object of study is not sufficient to justify the existence of an autonomous science of literature. For that we must prove not only that literature deserves to be known (a necessary condition) but that it is also absolutely different (a sufficient condition). Even further: as the object of a science is mainly delimited by the simplest categories and elements that constitute it, we must prove, in order to legitimate poetics as an autonomous science, that literary specificity is situated on a level already 'atomic," elementary, and not on a simply "molecular" level, the product of the combination of simpler elements.

Thus formulated, such a hypothesis remains, of course, possible; but it contradicts our everyday experience of literature. At whatever level we envisage it, literature possesses properties in common with other parallel activities. First of all, the sentences of a literary text already share the majority of their characteristics with all other discourse; but even their so-called specific features are to be found in puns, riddles, mnemonic devices, slang, etc. Less apparently, they communicate with pictural or gestural representation. On the level of the organization of discourses, the lyric poem shares certain properties with philosophic utterances; others, with prayer or with exhortation. Literary narrative, as we know, is close to that of the historian, of the journalist, of the witness. For the anthropologist, the role of literature is probably similar to that of the cinema, of the theater, more generally of all symbolism.

It is very possible that we can thus reconstitute a specificity of literature (variable with periods), but at a "molecular" level and no longer an "atomic" one. Literature will be a crossing of levels, which will not contradict the fact that on each of them its properties are shared by other productions. It is even possible (though I doubt it) that a certain property belongs only to literary texts; but how poor would be an image of literature consisting only of the common denominator of all literary texts, of what is only literature, compared with the image that unites everything that *can* be literature!

Hence the expression "science of literature" is doubly dismaying. There is not *one* science of literature, since, apprehended from different points of view, literature becomes the object of every other human science. Saussure had already noted as much apropos of language: "In order to assign a place to linguistics, we must not approach language from all its aspects. It is obvious that several sciences (psychology, physiology, anthropology, grammar, philology, etc.) could also claim language as their object." In the realm of literature, Jakobson also envisaged the possibility, for the other sciences, of "utiliz[ing] literary phenomena as documents of a defective and second-class variety. . . ." (p. 8). But, on the other hand, there is not a science of literature exclusively, for the features characterizing literature are to be found outside it, even if they form different combinations. The first impossibility relates to the laws of the discourse of knowledge; the second, to the particularities of the object studied.

We now see more clearly what has been and what must be the role of poetics. The refusal to know literature itself is only one particular case of a larger repression of all symbolic activity, which is translated by the reduction of the symbol to a pure function or to a simple reflection. That the reaction should have occurred first in literary studies rather than in those of myth or of rite, is the result of a combination of circumstances that it is history's task to elucidate. But today there is no longer any reason to confine to literature alone the type of studies crystallized in poetics: we must know "as such" not only literary texts but *all* texts,* not only verbal production but *all* symbolism.

---

*Our teaching still privileges literature, to the detriment of all other types of discourse. We must be aware that such a choice is purely ideological and has no justification in the phenomena themselves. Literature is inconceivable outside a typology of discourses.

Poetics is therefore called upon to play an eminently *transitional* role, even a transitory one: it will have served as an "indicator" of discourses, since the least transparent kinds of discourses are to be encountered in poetry; but this discovery having been made, the science of discourses having been instituted, its own role will be reduced to little enough: to the investigation of the reasons that caused us to consider certain texts, at certain periods, as "literature." No sooner born than poetics finds itself called upon, by the very power of its results, to sacrifice itself on the altar of general knowledge. And it is not certain that this fate must be regretted.

Bibliographical Note and Index

Bibliographical Note

I. Definition of Poetics

The modern usage of the word *poetics* can be traced through several authors: Paul Valéry, "On the Teaching of *Poetics* at the Collège de France in *Aesthetics*, trans. Ralph Manheim (New York: Bollingen Foundation, 1964), pp. 83-88; Roman Jakobson, "Linguistics and Poetics," originally in *Style in Language*, ed. Thomas A. Sebeok (Cambridge, Mass.: M.I.T. Press, 1960); Roland Barthes, *Critique et vérité* (Paris: Éditions du Seuil, 1966).

Friedrich Schlegel's thoughts on literature are found mostly in the fragments collected in the *Kritische Ausgabe* of his complete works. There is a convenient French translation: *L'Absolu Littéraire, Théorie Littéraire due Romantisme Allemand*, eds. Philippe Lacoue-Labarthe and Jean-Luc Nancy (Paris: Éditions du Seuil, 1978). The quotation from Henry James comes from his "Art of Fiction" published in *Selected Literary Criticism*, ed. Morris Shapiro (New York: McGraw-Hill Book Company, 1965), p. 58.

Jonathan Culler's *Structuralist Poetics* (Ithaca: Cornell University Press, 1971) gives another view of the general problems of poetics in recent literary theory. Periodicals such as *Poétique* (France); *Poetics* (Netherlands); *Poetik* (West Germany); *Poetics Today* (Tel Aviv); *New Literary History* (United States) and some others deal frequently with the fundamental problems of poetics.

Émil Benveniste, an influential French linguist of the postwar period, has published *Problèmes de linguistique générale* (Paris: Éditions Gallimard, 1966); English translation, *Problemes in General Linguistics*, trans. Mary Elizabeth Meek (Coral Gables: University of Miami Press, 1971) from which the quotation comes. Benveniste has also more recently published *Problèmes de linguistique générale II* (Paris, 1974). The American sociologist whom I quote is Erving Goffman, *Behavior in Public Places* (Free Press, 1963).

I owe special thanks to Ms. K. Jensen and to Mr. L. Waters for help in preparing this note.

II. Analysis of the Literary Text

i. Introduction: The Semantic Aspect

The reference to Aristotle is from the *Poetics,* of which numerous English translations exist, among others those by Hamilton Fyfe; Golden and Hardison; Else, etc. The last two include an extensive commentary. A new French translation of Aristotle followed by a four-hundred-page commentary was published in 1980 (Paris: Éditions du Seuil).

The rhetorical tradition can be studied through G. Kennedy's histories of Greek and Roman rhetoric or in some modern reinterpretations such as Jacques DuBois et al.: *Rhétorique générale* (Paris: Larousse, 1970); Christine Brooke-Rose, *A Grammar of Metaphor* (London, 1958). Other relevant studies of the mechanics of figurative meaning are to be found in William Empson, *The Structure of Complex Words* (London: Chatto and Windus, 1950); more recently, in R. M. Browne's "Typologie des signes littéraires," *Poétique,* 7, 1979. My *Symbolisme et interpétation* is a systematic presentation of the topic (Paris: Éditions du Seuil, 1978; English translation forthcoming: Cornell University Press).

The reference to Horace comes from *Ars Poetica.* A recent edition is *Satires, Epistles and Ars Poetica,* Loeb Classical Library, trans. H. R. Rairclough (1926; rpt. Cambridge: Harvard University Press, 1978).

Pierre-Daniel Huet's treatise is one of the first on the theory of the novel (a recent edition is Slatkine Reprints, Geneva, 1970). Chapelain was a theoretician of French Classicism; the reference to him is from *Les Sentiments de l'Académie française sur la tragi-comédie du Cid* (1638); in Armand Gasté, *La Querelle du Cid, pièces et pamphlets publiés d'après les origineaux* (Paris: 1898); also consult René Bray, *La Formation de la Doctrine Classique en France* (Paris: Librairie Nizet, 1963), p. 210. Saltykov-Shchedrin was a Russian satirical and realistic writer of the late nineteenth century whose statement on poetic verse was frequently quoted by the Russian Formalists. The reference to Frege is to his paper "Sense and Reference" in his *Philosophical Papers (Translations from the Philosophical Writings of Gottlieb Frege.* eds. Peter Geach and Max Black, Oxford: Blackwell, 1960).

Concerning Russian Formalists, the two basic collections in English are: *Russian Formalist Criticism,* eds. L. T. Lemon and M. J. Reis (Lincoln: University of Nebraska Press, 1965); *Readings in Russian Poetics,* eds. L. Matejka and K. Pomorska (Cambridge, Mass.: M.I.T. Press, 1971).

For the question of realism, refer to the recent issue of *Poétique,* 16, 1973 on "Le Discours réaliste."

One has the idea of the variety of approaches to the study of themes by consulting works as diverse as N. Frye, *Anatomy of Criticism* (Princeton, N.J.: Princeton University Press, 1957); G. Durand, *Les Structures anthropologiques de l'imaginaire* (Paris: Bordas, 1969), no English translation; R. Girard, *Deceit, Desire, and the Novel,* trans. Yvonne Freccero (Baltimore: Johns Hopkins Press, 1965); A. J. Greimas, *Sémantique structurale* (Paris: Larousse, 1966), no English translation; T. Todorov, *The Fantastic: a Structural Approach to a Literary Genre,* trans. Richard Howard (Ithaca, N.Y.: Cornell University Press, 1973).

The problems of interpretation are so all-pervasive to literary study that it is somewhat ridiculous to give a reading list. As an introduction to these problems, one could examine two recent issues of *New Literary History:* 3 (1972), 2; and 4 (1973), 2.

ii. Registers of Discourse

The definition of style as "register" can be found in *The Linguistic Sciences and Language Teaching* by M. A. K. Halliday, A. McIntosh, and P. Strevens (London, 1965), pp. 87-94.

Roman Jakobson deals with grammatical figures in "The Poetry of Grammar and the Grammar of Poetry," *Lingua*, 21 (1968), pp. 597-609. There is no convenient collection in English of his essays on literature so far, besides the early texts in *Readings in Russian Poetics*. A convenient French volume is *Questions de Poétique* (Paris: Éditions du Seuil, 1973).

Peirce's writings on symbols and signs are found in Volume 2 of his *Collected Papers* under the rubric "Speculative Grammar" (Cambridge, 1972). A classical treatise on rhetoric with a standard list of rhetorical figures is Quintillian's *Training of an Orator*, 4 vols., Loeb Classical Library, vols. 124-127 (Cambridge, Mass.: Harvard University Press).

On style as a deviation refer to S. Levin's studies, such as "Deviation—Statistical and Determinate—in Poetic Language" *Lingua*, 1963, pp. 276-90 or Jean Cohen's work done in France, *Structure du langage poétique* (Paris: Flammarion, 1966).

Shklovski's remark on the presence of the literary tradition comes from *Readings in Russian Poetics*. Bakhtin's most important book in English translation up to now is *Problems of Dostoevsky's Poetics*, trans. R. W. Rotsel (Ann Arbor: Ardis Publications, 1973). A new translation of this book is scheduled to appear from the University of Minnesota Press as a volume in the Theory and History of Literature series. Translations of his other books are forthcoming (e.g., University of Texas Press). My *Mikhail Bakhtin, Le principe dialogique* (Paris: Éditions du Seuil, 1981) presents systematically the theories of this most important twentieth-century literary critic.

Milman Parry's principal work is *The Making of Homeric Verse* (Oxford: Clarendon Press, 1971). Michael Riffaterre has published *The Semiotics of Poetry* (Bloomington: Indiana University Press, 1978) and *La Production du texte* (Paris: Éditions du Seuil, 1978, a different selection). Harold Bloom has a series of volumes on this topic starting with *The Anxiety of Influence* (New York: Oxford University Press, 1973). Bally's classic work is *Traité de stylistique française* (Geneva: Georg et Compagnie, 1951).

For Benveniste's ideas on "subjectivity" in language, consult his volume *Problems in General Linguistics*. A collection of essays from various authors in *L'Enonciation (Langages*, 17, 1970). Concerning emotive language, see E. Stankievicz, "Problems of Emotive Language" in Thomas A. Sebeok *et al.* (eds.) *Approaches to Semiotics* (The Hague: Mouton, 1964).

iii. The Verbal Aspect: Mode, Time

Roman Ingarden is a Polish philosopher, a disciple of Husserl who devoted several books, mostly in German, to the phenomenology of literature. In English, see *The Literary Work of Art*, trans. George G. Grabowicz (Evanston: Northwestern University Press, 1973).

In this chapter, I use some of the distinctions in Gérard Genette's study of the verbal aspect of narrative. See Genette's *The Narrative Discourse: an Essay in Method* (Ithaca: Cornell University Press, 1980), which is the most comprehensive and detailed presentation of the topic.

Some classic studies of time in literature are: G. Müller, "Erzählzeit und erzählte Zeit" in *Festschrift für P. Kluckhohn und H. Schneider* (1948, pp. 195-212); Käte Hamburger, *The Logic of Literature* (Bloomington: Indiana University Press, 1973); E.

Lämmert, *Bauformen des Erzählens* (Stuttgart: J. B. Metzlersche Verlagsbuchhandlung, 1955); A. A. Mendilow, *Time and the Novel* (London, 1952); D. Likhatchev, *Poètika drevnerusskoj literatury* (Leningrad, 1967), pp. 212-352; J. Ricardou, *Problèmes du nouveau roman* (Paris: Éditions du Seuil, 1967), pp. 161-71.

iv. The Verbal Aspect: Perspective, Voice

On the point of view, outside of Genette's synthesis, the standard studies are: Percy Lubbock's *The Craft of Fiction* (New York, 1921); Jean Pouillon, *Temps et Roman*, (Paris: Gallimard, 1946); Wayne Booth, *Rhetoric of Fiction* (Chicago: University of Chicago Press, 1962); Boris Uspenski, *A Poetics of Composition*, trans. Valentina Zavarin and Susan Wittig (Berkeley: University of California Press, 1973); Henry James, *The Art of the Novel* (New York: Charles Schribner's Sons, 1948). The notion of implied reader was introduced by Wayne Booth. See also Gerald Prince's study "Introduction à l'étude du narrataire" *Poétique*, 14, 1973, pp. 178-96.

v. The Syntactic Aspect: Structures of the Text

Tomashevski's suggestion about methodology comes from his "Thematics," translated in the Lemon and Reis anthology (pp. 60-95). On the notion of dominance, consult Roman Jakobson, "The Dominant" in *Readings in Russian Poetics*, (pp. 82-87).

My citation of E. M. Forster comes from the well-known *Aspects of the Novel*, cf. Chapter V, "The Plot" (New York: Harcourt, Brace, and World, Inc., 1927). The reference to Barthes is to his "An Introduction to the Structural Analysis of Narrative," in *New Literary History*, 6, 2 (Winter 1975), pp. 237-72.

The recent revival of plot study was initiated by the Russian folklorist V. J. Propp: *Morphology of the Folktale*, trans. Laurence Scott with introduction by Svatava Pirkova-Jakobson; 2d ed., revised ed. by Louis Wagner with introduction by Alan Dundes (Austin: University of Texas Press, 1968, 1st English ed., 1958); and *Selected Essays in Folklore*, trans. Richard and Ada Martin with introduction by Anatoly Liberman (Minneapolis: University of Minnesota Press, forthcoming). His work became well known among Western readers after Claude Lévi-Strauss's review of the English translation, "Structure and Form: Reflections on a Work by Vladimir Propp," *International Journal of Slavic Linguistics and Poetics*, 3 (1960). Propp was dissatisfied, however, with Lévi-Strauss's presentation and wrote a late rejoinder, translated in English as "Study of the Folktale: Structure and History" in *Dispositio* [Ann Arbor] 1 (1976), pp. 277-92.

The quotation from Jakobson comes from "Grammatical Parallelism and Its Russian Facet," *Language*, 42 (1966), pp. 339-429. But all of his studies of poetry illustrate this point. Joseph Frank's essay "Spatial Form in Modern Literature" is most easily accessible in his collection of essays, *The Widening Gyre* (New Brunswick, N.J.: Rutgers University Press, 1963), pp. 3-62.

vi. The Syntactic Aspect: Narrative Syntax

For an additional discussion of Vesselovski, Propp, and other forerunners of contemporary studies of plot structure see Claude Bremond, *Logique du récit* (Paris: Éditions du Seuil, 1973), which also presents Bremond's own views of narrative roles. For Shklovski's analysis of narrative, refer to the two anthologies of Russian Formalists previously mentioned. The reference to Tomashevski here is to his "Thematics," and that to Barthes is to his "An Introduction to the Structural Analysis of Narrative." Another attempt to formulate a "narrative grammar" is Gerald Prince's *A Grammar of Stories* (The Hague: Mouton, 1973).

III. Perspectives

i. Poetics and Literary History

Tynianov's fundamental essay of literary evolution is translated in *Readings in Russian Poetics*, (pp. 66-78). His study of parody was published in 1921 and his inquiry on the nature of the "literary fact" in 1925. No collection of Tynianov's writings on literature (which are among the most suggestive of Russian Formalist criticism) exists in English.

André Jolles's *Einfache Formen* was originally published by Max Niemeyer Verlag in 1929; this work, halfway between the study of folklore and the philosophy of literary forms, contains chapters on "Simple Forms" such as the riddle, joke, myth, legend, saga, etc.

E. Lämmert's discussion of the opposition between *genre* and type is in his *Bauformen des Erzählens* (pp. 9-18). An exemplary study of *genre* in French is the work of Phillippe Lejeune on autobiography; e.g. *Le pacte autobiographique* (Paris: Éditions du Seuil, 1974).

Hans Robert Jauss's essays dealing with the "horizon of expectation" have appeared lately in *New Literary History;* see also his "Theory of Genre and Medieval Literature" in *Toward an Aesthetic of Reception*, trans. Timothy Bahti with introduction by Paul de Man (Minneapolis: University of Minnesota Press, forthcoming). Various attempts have been made in recent years to infuse a new "poetic" blood in the old veins of literary history. *New Literary History*'s issues bear witness to some of these attempts.

ii. Poetics and Aesthetics

In using the term "the idea of beauty," I refer to Hegel's *Lectures on Aesthetics*, in particular, to volume 1.

Sartre's essay on Mauriac is in volume 1 of his *Situations;* English translation, "François Mauriac and Freedom" in *Literary and Philosophical Essays*, trans. Annette Michelson (London: Hutchinson and Co. Ltd., 1955), pp. 7-23.

Northrop Frye has vigorously denied literary studies their right to pronounce value judgments in the "Polemical Introduction" to his *Anatomy of Criticism* (Princeton, N.J.: Princeton University Press, 1957).

The relation between text and reader has become one of the most actively studied problems of literary theory in recent years. Consult *The Reader in the Text*, eds. Susan Suleiman and Inge Crosman (Princeton, N.J.: Princeton University Press, 1980), as well as the works of the Konstanz group of critics; among others: Wolfgang Iser, *The Act of Reading* (Baltimore: Johns Hopkins University Press, 1979); H. R. Jauss, *The Aesthetic Experience and Literary Hermeneutics*, trans. Michael Shaw (Minneapolis: University of Minnesota Press, forthcoming).

iii. Poetics as Transition

The essay of Jakobson is quoted in Eickenbaum's study translated in *Readings in Russian Poetics* (pp. 3-37). Saussure's remark comes from his *Course in General Linguistics*, trans. Wade Baskin (1959; rpt. New York: McGraw-Hill Book Co., 1966), p. 9.

Index

Tzvetan Todorov is Maître de Recherches at the Centre National de la Recherche Scientifique in Paris. Todorov, born and educated in Sofia, Bulgaria, has lectured at various North American universities. He has published ten books in French on literary theory, of which *The Poetics of Prose, The Fantastic: A Structural Approach to a Literary Genre,* and *Encylopedic Dictionary of the Sciences of Language* (with O. Ducrot) are in English.

Richard Howard is the author of *Untitled Subjects, Findings, Two-Part Inventions,* and other volumes of verse. He has written the critical study *Alone with America* and translated many texts from the French, including a number of those by Todorov and Roland Barthes.

Peter Brooks is Professor of French and Comparative Literature at Yale University. He is the author of *The Novel of Worldliness* and *The Melodramatic Imagination* and numerous essays.